2.

JANE AUSTEN'S
EMMA

A LANDMARK IN ENGLISH FICTION

TEXT AND CONTEXT

Editors

ARNOLD KETTLE
Professor of Literature
Open University

and

A. K. THORLBY
Professor of Comparative Literature
University of Sussex

◆

MICHAEL EGAN
Mark Twain's Huckleberry Finn:
Race, Class and Society

BERNARD HARRISON
Henry Fielding's Tom Jones:
The Novelist as Moral Philosopher

JEREMY HAWTHORN
Virginia Woolf's Mrs. Dalloway:
A Study in Alienation

DOUGLAS JEFFERSON
Jane Austen's Emma:
A Landmark in English Fiction

LAURENCE LERNER
Thomas Hardy's The Mayor of Casterbridge:
Tragedy or Social History?

Other Titles in Preparation

JANE AUSTEN'S
Emma

A Landmark in English Fiction

Douglas Jefferson

*Professor of English at
the University of Leeds*

SUSSEX UNIVERSITY PRESS

1977

Published for
SUSSEX UNIVERSITY PRESS
by

Chatto & Windus Ltd
40 William IV Street
London WC2N 4DF

*

Clarke, Irwin & Co Ltd
Toronto

Hardback ISBN 0 85621 058 7

Paperback ISBN 0 85621 059 5

©Douglas Jefferson 1977

Printed Offset Litho in Great Britain by
Cox & Wyman Ltd,
London, Fakenham and Reading

CONTENTS

INTRODUCTION

(1)

Jane Austen was a writer of fiction from her early teens; yet, like George Eliot, she did not publish any until her late thirties. Robert Liddell suggests that she would have liked 'to start life as a young author, like Fanny Burney,'[1] and regards early misadventures with publishers as fortunate in that they gave her reasons to wait and revise. Whatever her reasons for waiting the outcome places her in a very special category of novelists. Most novelists have written for immediate publication, whereas some of Jane Austen's novels appeared as much as sixteen years after what is taken to be the earliest version. This lapse of time must have made possible a reconsideration of the entire conception of a book, with a more concentrated quality in the writing. One of the remarkable virtues of her work is the resistance it offers on frequent re-reading, the growth in importance of details passed over in earlier readings, the wealth of significance to be found in the less conspicuous passages. Her novels in fact are very dense, and this would seem to be one consequence of long maturing.

Another consequence affects not only the individual work but also Jane Austen's general achievement in its relation to earlier phases of the novel. She began with parodies and burlesques, showing even as a child the liveliest sense of the ridiculous implications of fictional conventions, which she reduced to nonsense in the *jeux d'esprit* preserved in the three 'Volumes' of juvenilia. This was the beginning of an originality which was eventually to express itself in a new kind of novel. But the novels of earlier writers were her point of departure even in works where she approaches full maturity. Mrs Leavis has shown, for example, how much of *Pride and Prejudice* becomes more intelligible if we see it as a spirited response to Fanny

---

[1] *The Novels of Jane Austen*, London 1963, pp.xi-xii.

Burney's *Cecilia*. Elizabeth Bennet, in short, is an 'anti-Cecilia'.[2]
The reaction against eighteenth century modes and attitudes,
manifesting itself in this way, develops into a kind of 'realism'.
The anti-heroine differs from her predecessors simply in being
more like the girls we know. Catherine Morland, in *Northanger
Abbey*, is presented to us as a very ordinary girl, the ordinariness
comically stressed by way of allusion to the extraordinary perfections of earlier heroines; but soon she becomes quite an endearing person, low-keyed perhaps and with no special gifts,
touchingly inexperienced, but with a natural sense of correct
values; and it is satisfying that the much cleverer Henry Tilney
should appreciate her.

Under cover of parody and literary satire new types of character – heroines who are not paragons – could be developed. But
the new sense of reality brought new demands. The new heroine
might be somewhat imprisoned in a plot which travesties old
styles. Catherine Morland's ridiculous obsession with Udolpho-
like possibilities in the modern home of the Tilneys belongs too
much to parody and does an injustice to the otherwise sensible
little being whom we and the Tilneys have come to like.

The long delay in publication did not cause this particular
weakness in *Northanger Abbey* to be removed. Clearly the book
was a problem to her, and it might not have been published in
that form if she had lived. But in her most mature work, of which
Emma is a brilliant example, she was able to make fundamentally
original contributions to the art of the novel. We have no
evidence that *Emma* existed in an earlier version, though Mrs
Leavis has discussed very fully her use of ingredients from *The
Watsons*,[3] a fragment in manuscript of perhaps 1803 or somewhat later.[4] But the difference in conception and quality is
enormous. *The Watsons*, no doubt, was merely a draft, and surely
not of *Emma*. Jane Austen's dissatisfaction with the subject-
matter may be responsible for its incompleteness. We have no

[2] Q.D. Leavis, 'A Critical Theory of Jane Austen's Writings', in *Scrutiny*,
Vol. X, 1941. Reprinted in *A Selection from Scrutiny*, compiled by F.R.
Leavis, Vol, 2, London 1968.

[3] B.C. Southam criticises Mrs Leavis's view of the relationship between
The Watsons and *Emma* in *Jane Austen's Literary Manuscripts*, London
1964, Appendix.

[4] Southam discusses the date, *op.cit*., p.64.

knowledge of what a finished product of that phase of her development would have been like. It is not an especially early phase, but our disappointment with *The Watsons* may be explained, as Southam suggests, by the fact that she was suffering from 'a loss of creative power which may be related to the circumstances of her life at the time'.[5] She had no settled home, and residence in towns, after Steventon, was a kind of exile. Neither *The Watsons* nor *Lady Susan,* the manuscript of which belongs to the same period, gives us the remotest clue to her development at the level she was to achieve in her published work, which begins with *Sense and Sensibility* in 1811. Nor have we any clue to the remarkable advances in her art between *Sense and Sensibility* and *Pride and Prejudice* (1813), nor between these two novels and those that followed immediately afterwards: *Mansfield Park* (1814) and *Emma* (1815). The two earlier novels are those for which there is evidence of versions in the 1790s. They are nearer to the themes and methods of the eighteenth century, especially *Sense and Sensibility*, and this shows itself as a limitation. The later ones represent Jane Austen as the fully liberated artist, the totally successful exponent of a new fiction.

(2)

Jane Austen's originality will be a leading *motif* in this essay. It gives us a vantage point from which the novelists who precede her can be seen in a meaningful perspective, and those who come after in another. All great writers are very original, but their originality is not always noticed in one's early acquaintance with their works. It can easily be missed, and not always for the obvious reason that one knows too little about what went before. Knowing what went before may not always help very much. It helps one to see obvious and superficial kinds of newness, such as, for example, the fact that Walter Scott wrote about the past whereas his predecessors in fiction (except the authors of Gothic romances) wrote about their own society. This in itself does not make Scott the immensely original writer that he is. An original work is a new form of life, a new birth. The realisation that in a

---

[5] *Op.cit.*, p. 63.

certain book something has come into being quite different from what any earlier person achieved or imagined, may come to us long after the first enjoyable reading.

Originality may be of the spectacular kind, or it may be much less arresting. Scott's originality is spectacular. His ability to see communities in the process of historic change, and to show characters responding to the change and embodying it in their own changes of outlook was truly momentous. But spectacular though it is it went unrecognised until Georg Lukacs pointed it out in *The Historical Novel*. A spectacular achievement can go unnoticed, and Scott, who made this huge difference to the scope of the novel suffered scandalous neglect until comparatively recently.

Jane Austen's originality is of a much quieter kind, the opposite of spectacular, but as decisive as Scott's. And in a certain sense, which it will be possible to say more about later, it bears an interesting relationship to Scott's. Its precise character cannot be stated simply, but we may begin by looking back over the fiction of the eighteenth century. How does it all look? What observations can we make about it which we should not think of making if we did not enjoy the position of vantage which her works provide? The answer, or much of it, is glaringly obvious. These earlier works of fiction depend to an extraordinary extent on extreme situations. Tom Jones is expelled from his home, the victim of a wicked conspiracy. Smollett's heroes, Roderick Random and Peregrine Pickle, also have vicious enemies within their own families. Clarissa Harlowe is subjected to the most extreme family pressure to marry an odious suitor, and so, but without the same tragic consequences, is Sophia Western. The work of both Richardson and Fielding contains a great deal of sexual violence. Pamela's virginity is notoriously at risk. Clarissa, after escaping from her family, falls into the power of Lovelace who eventually rapes her. In *Sir Charles Grandison*, Richardson's least violent novel, a kidnapped heroine suffers rough handling as the bad baronet (the first of his kind) tries to bully her into a fraudulent marriage ceremony. The heroine of *Joseph Andrews*, after being rescued from sexual assault by Parson Adams, has to be rescued from kidnappers later in the story. Other forms of violence are equally common. Joseph Andrews is beaten up by footpads, Parson Adams participates in a glorious brawl. Smollett, the novelist with the most inveterate taste for violence, continually confronts his heroes with malignant enemies, presumably in order that the former may have frequent occasion for brutal reprisals. The comic element in some of these novels tends also to be extreme. Smollett was excessively fond of crude practical jokes. Novels of the road, where characters stay at inns, usually include one episode at least in which people get into the wrong bed, with embarrassing and sometimes violent consequences. It is a convention of this kind of fiction that heroes can never keep money. Black George robs Tom of his five hundred pounds. Captain Booth, in *Amelia*, falls in with gamblers and not only loses everything but comes away heavily in debt, while his faithful wife cultivates in exemplary fashion the virtues of simplicity and frugality. Roderick Random, upon his arrival in London, encounters coney-catchers who, after gaining his confidence, engage him in play and leave him penniless. The hero must always lose his money, because this is one of the ways in which the novel maintains its pattern of ups and downs. Extreme events were necessary to the eighteenth century novelist.

One way of ensuring that a novel is a history of ceaseless trial is to inflict on the heroine an impossible guardian or limit her freedom by an absurd will under which she must lose everything if she marries in the wrong circumstances. Of all the novels of the eighteenth century that depend on extreme situations a special prize must go to Fanny Burney's *Cecilia*. Fanny Burney has usually been viewed as Jane Austen's immediate predecessor, the novelist who helped her most, and Jane Austen expressed admiration for her. But nothing could be less like Jane Austen than the long sequence of exasperating and indeed horrifying events to which the poor heroine and the poor reader of this bulky novel are subjected. She has been given *three* guardians, all unsuitable for the most steeply contrasting reasons. She must stay with one of the three until she comes of age, the only one with whom it is feasible to stay being a man who lives for social entertainment and overspends his income. He puts Cecilia repeatedly under intolerable moral pressure to mortgage her future inheritance to pay his enormous debts, and eventually, when ruin can no longer be averted, commits suicide. Cecilia is loved, but by a young man whose family disapprove. (Her birth, 'though not contemptible, was merely decent'.) Mrs Leavis regards her lack of opposition to the noble Mrs Delvile, who appeals to her not to marry her son, as Jane Austen's target in the Lady Catherine de Burgh episode in *Pride and Prejudice*. Under the will by which she inherits her fortune, her husband, when he marries her, must take her name, otherwise she loses the money; and, of course, the man who loves her cannot possibly comply with such conditions. This is the sort of book in which a girl cannot show a charitable interest in a young man in misfortune without being suspected of another kind of interest; and once the misunderstanding sets in, it will be prolonged and renewed through a maddening succession of unlucky incidents. Her relationship with Delvile takes on the most tortuous and tormenting character. Gossips and impertinent questioners appear at precisely those moments when anxiety and the need for quiet and privacy are most acute. The heroine's trials are intensified, and before the end she is destitute and raving; but finally, released from her agonies, she is united to the man she loves, and the final chapter brings a very subdued happiness. In her *Diary* Fanny Burney quotes Francis Wyndham's complaint: 'How comes it that the moment you have attached us to the hero and heroine – the instant you have made us cling to them so that there is no getting disengaged – twined, twisted, twirled them round our very heart-string, – how is it that then you make them undergo such persecutions? There is really no enduring their distresses, their suspenses, their perplexities. Why are you so cruel to all around – to them and their readers?'[6] Fanny Burney's first book, *Evelina*, is less horrific, but also includes some extreme situations such as the exemplary episodes where the heroine suffers from the low manners of the Branghtons. The exemplary function of these passages is to illustrate all that vulgarity can do to embarrass a refined young lady, and the novelist misses no opportunity. The Branghtons are all vulgarity, Evelina all embarrassment, apprehension and wounded delicacy. Fiction like this has relations with the 'conduct book', and the characters are worked as hard as possible in the interest of particular moral or social points. In those parts of the book where Evelina experiences the importunities of the amorous Sir Clement, a conduct book lesson can again be learnt, a lesson in vigilance.

[6] *Diary and Letters of Madame D'Arblay*. Edited by her Niece (1842-6), Vol IV, p. 138.

Don't become detached from your party at Vauxhall.

Between Richardson and Jane Austen, with Fanny Burney as the connecting link, there is a decline in the magnitude of the risks to which heroines are exposed. Catherine Morland in *Northanger Abbey* has only the physically innocuous though very tiresome importunities of John Thorpe to fear. The danger is not abduction, but an unwanted ride in Thorpe's carriage, and the possibility of alienating more desirable friends. But the Thorpes have something of the menacing insistence of the tormentors in Fanny Burney's novels. John Thorpe causes Catherine to miss an engagement with the Tilneys by lying to her about their movements, and almost does it again by giving a lying message to the Tilneys about Catherine's 'previous engagement'. But whereas in Fanny Burney's world these misunderstandings cause prolonged misery, and the heroines have no plain commonsense course of action open to them − or so it seems − Catherine, as soon as Thorpe tells her of his visit to the Tilneys, breaks away from the company that tries to detain her, and in a great hurry makes her way to the Tilneys' lodgings, where out of breath she manages to explain the situation. There is a pleasing lack of stiffness in this solution. Catherine's trouble with the Thorpes may be regarded as an attenuated version of the troubles of her eighteenth century predecessors, but here we also detect the slightly humorous suggestion that in real life (Catherine, as we have seen, has been explicitly presented as no traditional heroine) the machinations of false friends can be thwarted if one is willing to make a dash for it and risk the minor indignity of being out of breath.

To say that Jane Austen's novels do not depend so much on extreme plot elements, that they are relatively quiet novels, would be to echo what everyone knows. This is only the superficial way of stating the difference between her work and that of her predecessors. But this point of difference has implications worth dwelling upon. The eighteenth century novel was not a vehicle for representing life as most people experience it most of the time, life in which the tensions and preoccupations are of the dimensions of the ordinary world. Jane Austen did more than anyone else to develop it in this direction. This was a major achievement, because it meant finding new ways of constructing novels and of making them interesting. Jane Austen was well equipped to do this, because plotting was one of her great arts;

but only in her mature works did she learn to build a plot with a significant and beautifully-ordered sequence of events, while maintaining throughout something very near to the logic of ordinary life. *Emma* is perhaps the best example of this achievement.

The difference has another aspect. In eighteenth century fiction one has no sense, as one does in Jane Austen, of particular stretches of time belonging to the characters ('their day') in which their role, whatever is happening in the story and it may be very little, is primarily that of being themselves. The events and characters tend to be conceived in accordance with some pattern or artifice. They have a role to sustain within a stylised sequence of actions and speeches. Cecilia, for instance, has no time to herself; she is entirely made over to the relentless scheme of events. Much of the cruelty of which readers of this novel complained lies in the claustrophobic network of contrived circumstances within which the heroine must play her strenuous exemplary role and outside which she cannot enjoy even the briefest period of free existence during which a reader could feel that she is 'there', to be known and recognised. Tom Jones, in many respects a live and human figure, or such is the impression successfully conveyed, becomes on inspection very much a creation of rhetoric, always the 'hero', with whatever accompaniments of literary style the particular episode calls for; and the style continually changes. Tom may be portrayed doing quite ordinary things, such as drinking beer (with Mrs Waters), but all is heightened by mock-heroic extravagance. On a serious occasion, as in the culminating scene with Sophia, the speeches are very formalised. He is wholly contained within this scheme of portrayal. The difference brought about by Jane Austen amounts to an advance in realism. The rhetorically conceived or idealised character was distanced by style and artifice. We are nearer to Emma, and Emma is nearer to human nature.

These changes affect both plot and character, the two aspects being difficult to keep apart. But as a matter of convenience it may be useful to concentrate on each of them in turn, and this will be the purpose of the two chapters that follow.

I

PLOT

(1)

The first chapter of *Emma* is entirely to our purpose. In a way that earlier fiction had no knowledge of this chapter deals primarily with a day in Emma's life: a very special day, because a crucial event has occurred: the marriage of Miss Taylor and Mr. Weston. But the event has occurred before we meet Emma, and the function of the chapter is to present Emma, reduced to her thoughts and to rather colourless routine activities. She has dinner with her father, who then falls asleep, and she now has nothing to do but 'sit and think of what she had lost'. It had been 'a black morning's work for her. The want of Miss Taylor would be felt every hour of every day'. How was she to bear it? Tea comes, and her father renews with her the regrettable topic. Fortunately a visitor appears, Mr Knightley. He is a regular visitor, being not only a good neighbour but also Emma's brother-in-law; already one of the family. Mr Woodhouse thanks him for calling, deploring only the shocking weather. It is, in fact, as Mr Knightley says, 'a beautiful, moonlight night'. The marriage becomes once again the subject for talk. Mr Woodhouse begs his daughter to do no more match-making. Mr Knightley expresses scepticism about the importance of her role as match-maker in the recent case, while Emma pleads for one more try, on behalf of 'poor Mr Elton'.

Those readers who associate Jane Austen's novels with the limited concerns of the drawing room and the tea table, will find support here, but such criticism misses the important point. The novel begins, as earlier novels did not, with the central figure simply living her life, in a setting recognisably everyday. The day has given her new facts to digest, but as she ponders alone, presides over tea or chats with her father and their visitor, she is just 'being herself', and we can begin to know her. Situations by no means lacking in piquancy, tension and mystery will develop in subsequent chapters, but they will arise out of those everyday activities in which the characters have little more to do than respond to the familiar facts of their world. The familiarity of it all is an ever-present fact throughout the book. In *Emma* all events, including the climactic ones, come about in the course of everyday living, and partake of its tone. Most of them are events in her experience. There are, of course, passages of another kind, such as Chapter 2, which consists of a backward glance over the life of Mr Weston and gives us the first mention of Frank; and occasionally, but very rarely, a scene takes place from which Emma is excluded, as in Chapter 5. But in general the novel is about Emma whom we know through a sequence of events the character of which is that, though they may advance the plot, they are in the first place events in her day to day existence.

This pattern of opening, new in *Emma*, has been much repeated, and in our time has almost become a commonplace. To take a very modern example, almost at random, Iris Murdoch's *An Unofficial Rose* begins with an episode in the life of a central character, Hugh Peronett, an elderly man. He is, in fact, attending his wife's funeral and reflecting on a variety of loosely related topics mainly concerned with himself, his marriage, members of the family who are present and whom he observes, and one other person, a woman with whom long ago he had an affair and who now unexpectedly turns out to be present. The chapter has a generally introductory function, but central to it is our sense of Hugh living through this particular stretch of time (the words of the burial service are there to punctuate it and prompt his reflections), and of the tone and temper of his mind, which the novelist allows us to savour at leisure. Certain characteristics begin to manifest themselves, but not sharply. Hugh cherishes in a mild way the feeling that his life, his married life in particular, has gone by without undue disturbance. In an Iris Murdoch novel we know from this that there are some surprises ahead. An opening on these lines is common in Agatha Christie's detective stories, where one person and his or her impressions and memories, perhaps at the beginning or end of a family occasion, serve to provide a human centre and to introduce the scene and background of the events which are to follow. Twentieth century novelists like Virginia Woolf in *Mrs Dalloway* have carried much further the technique of introducing us to a character living through a particular day. In this book the events are in fact limited to the one day, and the novelist's main concern would seem to be to capture the moment by moment responses of the central figure to stimuli that follow each other with something of the haphazardness and the ordinariness of real life. There are, in fact, rhythms and patterns, the day takes a shape, and the lyrical style from the outset has a vitalising and harmonising effect on the otherwise desultory and disjointed items of experience. This, of course, takes us a long way from the first chapter of *Emma*: but perhaps the first chapter of *Emma* may be seen also as the first chapter of the history (or of *a* history) of modern fiction, pointing forward to developments such as these.

More immediately it points forward to openings in George Eliot and Henry James. *Middlemarch*, after the introductory account of Dorothea's slightly eccentric, aspiring nature, (one might contrast this with the bland and easy 'Emma Woodhouse, handsome, clever and rich. . .') opens with her return home from a visit to the infant school she had 'set going' and the scene that follows with her sister Celia. They talk about their late mother's jewels, which Celia thinks should now be looked at and divided among themselves, but to which Dorothea has not give a thought. Idiosyncrasy is more on display than in the first chapter of *Emma*, but the effect here, and in the next chapter (the dinner party with Mr Casaubon), is similar in that we are being taken through a day in the heroine's life and her words and actions are such as will convey to us the tone of her everyday outlook and behaviour, so that we may immediately begin to know her. But Dorothea differs from Emma in having no interest in the domestic and the social as such, so that we cannot begin with a scene in low relief, as it were. If this were the place for a comparison between Jane Austen and George Eliot one might argue that the latter, the more ambitious novelist, involves her heroine in more adventures than she is prepared to bring within the compass of the everyday consciousness. Up to a point we follow her in her first reactions to Mr Casaubon, but soon we shall not be with her at all. What do we know, for example, of her ideas about the (presumably) sexless marriage she enters upon? Jane Austen so planned her book that all Emma's actions and preoccupations can be made known to the reader; and we are with her in all the crises of her life. Lionel Trilling, in his essay on *Emma*, asks why (echoing a remark by Newman) we feel 'kind to the heroine, in spite of so much', and a part of his answer is that 'we come into

17

an unusual intimacy with her. We see her in all the elaborateness of her mistakes, in all the details of her wrong conduct. The narrative technique of the novel brings us very close to her and makes us aware of each misstep she will make.'[1] The narrative technique to which he refers includes the feature we have been examining: the placing of all events within a framework of familiar, day-to-day activities. Henry James, another novelist who is more ambitious than Jane Austen, and nearer to George Eliot, can give the reader something of the same feeling of intimacy with a heroine, and of apprehension concerning her ignorance and her errors. But Isabel Archer, like Dorothea Brooke but more so, does many important things which are not directly shown. When we do see her, and share her consciousness, accompanying her, for example, to Lockleigh, Lord Warburton's home or to Osmond's villa, visits which for such a person are explorations of unknown human territory, James can achieve great inwardness. But we are not quite near enough to Isabel when she draws near to the biggest decision of her life, the marriage with Osmond, or during whole years after it has been made. There is much to be said for a novel like *Emma* in which everything important in the heroine's conduct is seen in the light of common day. The openness of Emma's character, and the openness of Jane Austen's presentation of it, combine to give this novel one of its great attractions. Inevitably the nineteenth century novelist had to go further, and the twentieth century novelist further still, in the exploration of human problems, and the results have been most impressive; but there was one accompanying condition, and that was the likelihood that the problematic situation would only be incompletely presented, with crucial aspects not presented at all. It was a sign of growth that the novel should go beyond the age-old convention whereby stories end with marriage, and should attempt to portray marriage itself with its cheats and painful discoveries. Some of the greatest novels in the language are about women who, through some strange error and fault of character, find themselves married to a gross egoist or an emotional cripple. In the subtle portrayal of these women and their husbands the

---

[1] '*Emma* and the Legend of Jane Austen', originally an Introduction to Riverside edition of *Emma*, New York, 1957; reprinted in Casebook series, *Emma*, ed. David Lodge, London 1968, pp.158-9.

English novel takes a step forward, yet something is missing. Gwendolen Harleth, on the day when she accepts Grandcourt in Chapter 27 of *Daniel Deronda*, is known to us in the way Emma is known to us when she flirts with Frank Churchill at Box Hill, and in both cases one can refer to the heroine's 'day', as well as to the particular event. But after the marriage a good deal disappears from our view. Conventional exclusions of sexual relations must be accepted in novels of that period, but here we actually remain in ignorance of matters essential to our reading of the situation and of the characters involved. Was Gwendolen, for example, unable to respond sexually after the shock inflicted by Mrs Glasher's letter? And later? How far was the 'mastery' of her which Grandcourt so desired primarily a matter of physical possession, and if so was he thwarted, or was he so tired of sex (in his mid-thirties?) that quelling her spirit was satisfaction enough? What we are told gives no clue to their relationship, and a variety of guesses would be possible. This must surely be regarded as a flaw. At the end of the book we know Gwendolen less well than in the earlier part.

(2)

Emma is one of the best plotted novels in the language, but a number of its earlier readers, including intelligent and admiring ones, saw it as uneventful and lacking in plot. Susan Ferrier found it 'excellent' but added '. . . there is no story whatever'. Newman noted 'a want of body to the story'. W.D. Howells said that the action was 'slight. . . the story makes its round with a few events so unexciting as to leave the reader in doubt whether anything at all has happened', and he went on to specify 'duels and abductions', the machinery of eighteenth century fiction, as events missing from her work.[2] These curious comments give something of the measure of the newness of Jane Austen's methods. Because the action of her novels takes place within a framework of merely social events — a dinner party, a ball, a summer outing, a morning visit to friends — because the tone of the narrative is adjusted so nearly to that of lives in which these are landmarks, readers failed

[2] *Emma*, in Casebook series, ed. David Lodge, pp.49-62.

to recognise the intricate and significant structure of the plot which unfolds itself in the course of this sequence of Highbury activities.

For all her great skill in plotting, it took Jane Austen some time to discover the right kind of plot for her subject-matter, and it may help to establish a perspective if we begin by looking at *Sense and Sensibility*, which may almost be regarded as an exemplary case of what to avoid. In this novel, immature in conception, she had not taken the measure of her special problems as a novelist, and the oddities in its structure may help us to see what those problems were. The two sisters, Elinor and Marianne, it will be remembered, are living in reduced circumstances with their mother in a new home in Devonshire. Two gentlemen (who are eventually to marry them) visit the neighbourhood at different times. These are Edward Ferrars, who has shown affection for Elinor, which she would willingly return; and Colonel Brandon, an older man, in love with Marianne, to whose ardent nature he makes no appeal. A third gentleman also comes their way as a result of an accidental encounter. Marianne damages her ankle, a debonair young man called Willoughby comes to her aid, carries her home, and here begins the friendship which is to cost her so much emotional suffering. Let us briefly summarise certain events in the order in which they occur, with some indication of their timing. We begin with Colonel Brandon, who has planned an excursion for the two sisters, Willoughby and the Middletons with whom he is staying. At the beginning of Chapter 13 the post arrives and Brandon gets a letter which causes him great consternation. He must depart immediately. The excursion is off, to everyone's disappointment including the reader's, because now we have a non-event instead of the kind of event that Jane Austen could do very well. The reason for Brandon's departure remains a secret. Chapter 15 begins with Marianne in tears. Willoughby has received orders from his rich kinswoman, Mrs Smith, and he too must depart. What he says about not returning for a long time, and his confused manner of speech, makes the occasion especially unhappy and ominous. Again there are no explanations. But in the next chapter Edward Ferrars appears. He is not in good spirits and, although there is a renewal of friendship with the sisters, clearly something is weighing on his mind. After a week he says he must go. He has no wish to go, no commitments elsewhere, his time is his own, but still he must go, and the sisters are not to know why. We have now reached Chapter 19. Three unexplained departures in seven chapters!

What happens then when visits are broken off and situations involving young women and their men friends are left mysteriously inconclusive? There are other sources of interest, of course. Lady Middleton's sister and brother-in-law, the Palmers, arrive, and this provides an opportunity for some amusing characterisation. Then the two sisters are taken to London, and this leads to Marianne's unhappy confrontation with Willoughby and her prolonged illness. But it takes some time for the mysteries to be cleared up, and this necessitates a certain amount of retrospective narration (in the eighteenth century manner) dealing with events which, though crucial in their effect on the relations of the main characters, must remain very distant from the restricted world of experience of the person who receives these narratives; that is, Elinor, who is the centre of consciousness in *Sense and Sensibility*. A seduction and a duel have taken place, both very far in time and place from her sheltered, domestic life. One of the peculiarities of the novel is that, like the eighteenth century fiction we have noted, it depends in some measure on extreme events; but they belong to the periphery of the story, insofar as Elinor, at the centre, can learn of them only by report and long after they have occurred. Elinor's access to the most important factors in the lives of the menfolk, which are of great importance to her sister and herself, is irritatingly deferred and limited in value. In general this novel suffers from an impoverishment in the central area of the action, the heroine's area.

Sense and Sensibility, admirable though so much of it is, might almost have been written to demonstrate the possible inconveniences of seeing everything from the point of view of women whose role in society is static and domestic, so that they are entirely dependent on the men if anything is to happen. The visit of a man is an event; but if he goes, especially if he gives no reasons, there is a hold-up, the movement of the book may be halted or slowed down, and the structure may become rather broken-backed. Both we and the heroines are left dependent on the next male character to provide another event.

Jane Austen's need then was to choose and arrange situations so that her heroine, however limited to the domestic and social

21

role, is continuously engaged in a sequence of events that doesn't flag or suffer awkward interruptions. The older novelists could keep interest lively by causing the men to apply extreme and repeated pressure, but Jane Austen forgoes this resource. Ravishers, kidnappers, monstrous parents and guardians are excluded. Using as her central figures young women living quietly at home, not exposed to exceptional dangers and excitements, and limiting herself to their point of view on the action, she had the problem of inventing an action which would give them scope. A Jane Austen novel, if it is to have richness and density, needs a plot which will occupy the heroine all the time in situations which bring the opposite sex into play. Already one can see how convenient it is that Mr Knightley should be related by marriage to the Woodhouses, so that in that first chapter and many subsequent chapters he can, quite naturally, have conversations with the heroine and develop the relationship which, late in the book and quite suddenly, is to become everything to her. Equally convenient, from the point of view of the plot, is Emma's special relationship with the Westons, which makes her ready for a special relationship with Frank Churchill. Frank must be ranked among the absentee males during the first part of the novel, but he makes an appearance just at the point when the plot needs him, after Emma's plans for Harriet have broken down and she is left without an interest. But the plot is also served by the central fact that Emma, with an active temperament and 'a disposition to think rather too well of herself', needs scope for her powers after the marriage of Miss Taylor to Mr Weston. Her adoption of Harriet follows as a consequence. She is in a position to adopt her, and to introduce her to good society. As her father's daughter she can provide a setting in which the comedy of Harriet, Mr Elton and herself can develop through a sequence of informal meetings at Hartfield. The plot advances naturally with the alternation of scenes with Harriet and Mr Elton and scenes where Mr Knightley, and also his brother visiting with the family from London, provide a contrasting note, the note of disapprobation and warning. The alternation is made easy by the social facts of Emma's existence. Mr Knightley can appear whenever he pleases. After the seventh chapter, dominated by Emma's awful folly, we have one in which the whole situation involving Harriet and Robert Martin receives, on the following day, a drastic

22

reinterpretation from an angry and formidably intelligent Mr Knightley; and now that Emma has committed herself as fully as possible to the direction of Harriet's life, and our sense of her wrongness has been intensified by Mr Knightley's judgment, a chapter immediately follows in which we have a sample of what she is doing for the intellectual improvement of her young *protegée*, the chapter about the collection of riddles. The sequence has a moral shape, and irony builds up as Emma continues with her delusion. Then the sardonic comments of Mr John Knightley on Mr Elton's interest in *her*, followed by Mr Elton's curious indifference to Harriet's illness and absence from dinner at Randalls, prepare her in some measure for the prodigious scene in the coach. The point here is not just that Jane Austen has plotted these chapters very piquantly, but the more elementary, though fundamental one, that she has selected and placed her heroine in such a way as to make a rich and varied involvement possible. It seems appropriate to such a writer that her artistic triumphs should have their roots in common sense.

After the Elton fiasco the novel enters into a new phase with new characters, and the plotting becomes extraordinarily dense. Before we try to examine it in some detail perhaps it would be useful to dwell a little longer on this elementary matter of Jane Austen's choice and placing of her heroine in the mature novels. The planning of *Mansfield Park*, from this point of view, is quite different, less intricate but also highly successful; and indeed the action of that novel can be viewed very largely in terms of such basic arrangements. Here the character from whose point of view virtually everything is seen is Fanny Price, unlike Emma in having the least reason for self-confidence and assertiveness of all the people in the book. But she is wonderfully well placed as the reflector of the life around her. Always vulnerable, she can measure with her own sensibility the exact degree of other people's kindness or unkindness. Edmund shows her much kindness, but when Mary Crawford monopolises his attention Fanny loses her riding exercise as well as feeling generally a little hurt and jealous. The young people of Mansfield Park become known to us in relation to the contrasting influences brought to bear upon them: the dignified but too remote influence of Sir Thomas, the active and vicious partiality of Mrs Norris, and the indolence of Lady Bertram, who is only an influence in that there is something missing which ought to be there. The seed sown by Mrs Norris has every opportunity to produce an interesting harvest when the Crawfords appear, and Henry Crawford flirts with both of the Bertram sisters. Fanny's merits as a reflector are enhanced by her being less of a participant, more of a spectator than the others; though in the private theatricals sequence pressures are brought to bear upon her to participate, so that her awareness of something wrong in the behaviour of the others becomes also a personal drama, especially as the dilemma of Edmund — *his* drama — becomes Fanny's also, because she loves him and he loves Mary. A good example of Jane Austen's careful arrangement of circumstances follows after this episode. Maria Bertram marries Mr Rushworth and her sister Julia goes to stay with the married couple. It is as simple as that, but it enables Fanny to move into the front line. The timing is most appropriate. Fanny has just reached the stage when people begin to notice her good looks, and Sir Thomas wants to do something in her honour. He gives her a ball. But Henry Crawford, deprived of the Bertram sisters, also begins to notice Fanny, whose change of status now leads to a new kind of importance in the plot. Fanny has to suffer a severe trial when she refuses Henry Crawford's offer of marriage and Sir Thomas, greatly dismayed, feels that it is time for her to get her proportions right. She must return to her Portsmouth home for a while. Jane Austen gets her proportions right. The degree of pressure exerted by Sir Thomas, and the space given to this crisis, are just as they should be. We do not return to the rigours of eighteenth century confrontations. The visit to Portsmouth is well devised. It offers a new focus of interest at a point in the novel where otherwise there could only have been uncomfortable suspense, with Fanny holding out and Sir Thomas displeased. But the Portsmouth home is depressing and limiting, and the novel could have flagged if Fanny had simply been obliged to wait there until circumstances at Mansfield changed. But no, Henry Crawford follows her to Portsmouth, he behaves well — he has been getting better and better since he fell in love with Fanny — so Fanny's problem never ceases to be lively. Her trial is timed to end when Henry's elopement with Maria justifies her in her refusal to marry him, and the misbehaviour of both of the Bertram sisters places Fanny now in a special position in another and more important sense at

Mansfield Park and in relation to Sir Thomas. Henry's elopement has the immediate effect of ending Mary's friendship with Edmund, so that the way now becomes clear for Edmund to discover that Fanny is the girl he must marry. The plot may be seen then as a sequence of groupings and re-groupings of characters, with a gradual clearing of the scene to make way for Fanny, who has now earned the central place. Her progress gives no pleasure to certain readers, but her defence will not be attempted here. The relevant point for this discussion concerns technique, Jane Austen's art in keeping her heroine occupied in a succession of fruitful situations, which test and develop her character, and which combine to form a significant and shapely whole. *Mansfield Park* lends itself more easily than *Emma* to brief analytical description. It has a very clear and satisfying outline.

If *Mansfield Park* and *Emma* are both splendid examples of plotting, but, in the first place, examples also of wise placing of the heroine, *Pride and Prejudice* has something in common with *Sense and Sensibility*, though greatly superior to it. Again the heroine and her sister are fully occupied in a developing situation when the gentlemen are near at hand, but are somewhat at a loss when they depart without explanation. As in *Sense and Sensibility*, subsidiary interests help to fill the gap. Charlotte Lucas marries Mr Collins, the Gardiners make their appearance, Elizabeth visits Charlotte in her new home and receives an invitation to dine with Lady Catherine, and so forth; and before long she has another encounter with Mr Darcy. We need not complain. With Elizabeth interest can hardly be said to flag, and the effect of the departure of the Netherfield party does not have quite the disruptive effect of the three successive departures in the earlier novel. But compared with the later books *Pride and Prejudice* has rather a lack of roundedness, and of density of composition. With the centre of consciousness located as usual in the heroine it has rather too many events that depend on the male characters and cannot be shown as part of her experience. A good deal of her experience must take the form of waiting. In spite of all that Elizabeth's personality can do a certain deficiency of action may be felt in the later stages of the book. Once the crisis caused by Lydia's elopement with Wickham has been dealt with, and Mr Darcy has been revealed in his new role as a true friend to the Bennets, there are only a few foregone conclusions to be settled. The gentlemen have returned and marriages are to be arranged. But all this takes time, and the slowness is Mr Darcy's slowness. When everything depends on the man and the man is slow, what can the heroine or the reader do but wait? In Chapter 54, where Mr Darcy has dinner with the Bennets, Elizabeth feels that now, if ever, he will say something:

> She was in hopes that the evening would afford some opportunity of bringing them together; that the whole of the visit would not pass away without enabling them to enter into something more of conversation, than the ceremonious salutation attending his entrance. Anxious and uneasy, the period which passed in the drawing room, before the gentlemen came, was wearisome and dull to a degree, that almost made her uncivil. She looked forward to their entrance, as the point on which all her chance of pleasure for the evening must depend.
>
> 'If he does not come to me, *then*', said she, 'I shall give him up for ever.'

And, of course, he fails to do so. The wearisomeness and dullness continue for Elizabeth, and for the reader too the chapter has not been one of the best.

(3)

The second phase of *Emma* occupies Chapters 17 to 47, and then the plot as an intricate structure comes to an end, though there still remain some important matters, including Emma's final understanding with Mr Knightley, to be transacted. The plotting here is of a very high order indeed, and involves the interweaving of a number of themes and situations which need to be disengaged and examined if we are to appreciate the fullness of the whole. In the first place it may be useful to stress that Emma's matchmaking does not rank among the more important of these themes. After the Elton episode she foreswears match-making, and her words to Harriet (in Chapter 40) when she supposes that Frank may be the object of a new interest, are quite cautious. In Chapter 43, at Box Hill, she misinterprets some words of his (about her choice of a wife for him) as alluding to Harriet, but this goes no further than her thoughts. So, although she feels distressed and guilty when Frank's secret engagement becomes known and Harriet's feelings are once again a matter for concern (in Chapter 47), it can hardly be said that she has done much to mislead her this time. Emma is, in fact, beset by other dangers, and these build up gradually as several new characters appear, each of them the source of a special temptation or threat.

The first of the new characters to be awaited, though not the first to arrive, is Frank Churchill. His letter of excuse, which brings disappointment to the Westons, and provokes the severe criticism of Mr Knightley, provides the subject matter of Chapter 18. 'His letters disgust me', says Mr Knightley, which implies that in this limited community a letter may be passed round or, at least, quoted fully. The question of the size of the community and of the range of possibilities, or duties, it affords to members, Emma in particular, is of recurring importance throughout this part of the novel. Frank's visit, she reflects, would mean, 'an addition to their confined society in Surry; the pleasure of looking at some body new'. Her thought of 'the gala-day to Highbury entire, which the sight of him would have made', suggests amusement at the way it might go to other heads than her own. At this point in the story Emma does not feel very strongly about Frank's failure to arrive, except as a disappointment for the Westons: 'She wanted rather to be quiet and out of temptation'. In general one has the impression that Emma has never had strong cravings for an enlarged circle, and that before the aboriginal misfortune that robbed her of the constant companionship of Miss Taylor all was well. (On the other hand, after Frank's visit and sudden departure, in Chapter 30, Emma feels 'a sad change', as she returns to the 'common course of Hartfield days'. How and with whom to occupy her time: she might well be conscious of this as her problem after two such lively weeks). Chapter 19 presents another aspect of this general theme. Emma's need to put an end to Harriet's doleful chat about Mr Elton, as they walk out together, causes her to do something that she does very infrequently, and indeed that she is criticised for not doing often enough. She calls, with Harriet, on Mrs and Miss Bates. They arrive at a moment auspicious for these good simple people. Another letter has arrived and must be made public, Jane's letter announcing her forthcoming visit. Emma hears the main substance of the letter, but leaves in time to avoid the whole recital. We learn that her visits are infrequent because she finds the Bateses 'tiresome' and because of 'all the horror of being in danger of falling in with the second rate and third rate of Highbury, who were calling on them for ever'. Whatever must be said about this element of unkindness to the Bateses — and it culminates in the event that brings about her deepest humiliation — it may be necessary for modern readers, accustomed to greater mobility and more freedom in choosing friends and associates, to use their imagination a little on Emma's behalf. Emma is 'clever', to use one of the opening epithets of the novel, and no one can accuse her of being, on that account, restless or difficult. On the contrary, she looks after her old father with perfect good nature and asks for very little in life, though that little includes having the initiative in matters she has decided opinions about, such as Harriet's prospects. Mr Woodhouse has no exclusiveness in him, largely because he has little capacity for criticism, and it falls to Emma's lot frequently to round up such ladies as Mrs Goddard and the Bateses for an evening at Hartfield, where she cheerfully provides them with rather better fare than her father, with his valetudinarian anxieties, could have conscientiously recommended. But their 'quiet prosings' are a trial to her.

Emma has a preference for a certain kind of company: in short, for the best, but this simple fact can easily be misread, as the difference between this kind of company and other kinds happens largely to coincide with a difference of class. She has benefited from an early age not only from the excellent companionship of Miss Taylor, but also from the supreme influence of Mr Knightley, a man of sense as well as a gentleman, in every way the most impressive person in Highbury. Only at a late stage in the story does the full importance of this influence come home to her: 'Mr Knightley must marry no one but herself.' Until this point love has not been in her mind. The question of what company she should keep, a question of social ethics, takes its special form for her because of Mr Knightley. We need think only of the father of Anne Elliott in *Persuasion* to see how far Jane Austen could be from linking social rank with other forms of superiority, but Emma takes Highbury as she finds it, and in Mr Knightley and his brother the link does exist. Her rather sentimental ideas about gentility, as expressed in the celebrated passage in Chapter

42 conveying her thoughts at Donwell Abbey, are relevant here:

> ... It was just what it ought to be, and it looked what it was —
> and Emma felt an increasing respect for it, as the residence of
> a family of such true gentility, untainted in blood and under-
> standing. Some faults of temper John Knightley had; but
> Isabella had connected herself unexceptionably. She had given
> them neither men, nor names, nor places, that could raise
> a blush.

'Blood' and 'understanding' are bracketed together.

Emma's exclusiveness is a complex theme, not very easy to
discuss precisely. When the Coles propose to give a dinner (Chapter 25) her reaction takes a form which readily earns the epithet
'snobbish'. The Coles, though 'very good sort of people' are of
'low origin, and only moderately genteel'. They 'ought to be
taught that it was not for them to arrange the terms on which
the superior families should visit them.' But after the comedy
of the invitations Emma gladly goes to the dinner, to which all
her friends, including Mr Knightley, are also going. She enjoys
it, and the next day takes pleasure in the thought of her 'condescension' and the 'worthiness' of the Coles. At first sight the
moral would seem to be obvious. But what of the dinner itself?
The guests include 'the male part of Mr Cox's family', and this
reminds us of William Cox, the 'pert young lawyer' whom Emma
(Chapter 16) thought of and then rejected, with a laugh and a
blush, as a possible substitute for Mr Elton as Harriet's suitor.
The level of conversation seems commonplace:

> ... a few clever things said, a few downright silly, but by
> much the larger proportion neither the one nor the other—
> nothing worse than every day remarks, dull repetitions, old
> news, and heavy jokes.

Emma's first response to a situation like this is resistance, but in
the end she goes along with arrangements in which her friends
show the way. Highbury society can hardly be accused of exclusiveness. The party would not have been very enjoyable if her
frineds had not been present. Her standard may relate specifically to gentility, but surely the association for her between
gentility and certain qualities of mind and outlook are relevant.

An analogous situation arises in the passage (Chapter 24)

where Frank Churchill begins to be interested in the Crown as a place for dancing. The 'highest purpose' for which anyone now uses this inn is 'to accommodate a whist club established among the gentlemen and half-gentlemen of the place.' Our difficulty here may be to interpret the word 'half-gentlemen'. Does it mean pretentious persons, embarrassing parvenus, 'pert young lawyers' or people worthy of respect but of rather less consequence than Mr Knightley, Mr Weston and others? Frank's scheme will need numbers, and in a district with such a want of 'proper families' the company will perhaps have to include some of the 'half-gentlemen', in the sense that includes the pert young lawyer. Emma feels some discomfort over his 'indifference to a confusion of rank', which 'bordered too much on inelegance of mind.' But when the time comes the party does indeed include William Cox and other lesser figures of the community, and again Emma has no inclination to make objections. The dance is in her honour, and she enjoys it very much. Frank behaves in his most charming and friendly manner, and she only regrets that Mr Knightley 'could love a ballroom better, and could like Frank Churchill better'.

Emma then has only a limited choice of the company she keeps. In general she likes to go where her friends go, though perhaps after suppressing an initial preference for a smaller circle. To go back to Chapter 19 and Jane Fairfax's imminent visit: this addition to Highbury society will mean two things for Emma; two things which in that small, narrowly defined world cannot be escaped. One, there will be more occasions on which Mrs and Miss Bates will be present; and the other, she will need to make another effort to give her friendship to Jane. She cannot like Jane, but recognises her duty to her, while resenting the assumption that as girls of the same age they should be friends. Jane's superiority to her in artistic accomplishments makes the situation more embarrassing. How unfortunate that in her first conversation with Emma, on her arrival (Chapter 20), Jane, as she confesses later, feels that she must act a part, and replies to her questions with more than her usual reserve and aloofness. So the friendship does not develop.

This part of the novel, beginning with the arrival of Jane, followed by that of Frank (the timing becomes more apparent later) and the dinner at the Coles, is characterised by increasing sociability. The few dances at the end of the Coles' party sets Frank's mind working towards a continuation, originally conceived as taking place at Randalls and then developing into the larger project which, after some delay, takes place at the Crown. Discussion of this scheme occupies Chapter 29, but Frank's summons to return to Mrs Churchill comes in the next chapter. Unlike *Sense and Sensibility* the novel does not lose momentum at this sudden departure. Other pressures will soon be felt. Mr Elton brings his bride to Highbury, and the advent of Mrs Elton is the occasion for a frenzied development of social activity. Emma's intense dislike of her begins with the first exchange of visits, during which she has every kind of evidence of her vulgarity, but as all Highbury seems to be conspiring not to allow the Eltons a single free day, she realises that there can be no escape for her: 'They must not do less than the others, or she should be exposed to odious suspicions, and imagined capable of pitiful resentment. A dinner there must be.' This affords her an opportunity to include Jane Fairfax, about whom she has been feeling guilty. The occasion is the most fully treated episode in the novel, extending over Chapters 34 to 36, and in the last of these chapters Mr John Knightley makes a remark which, like his other remarks, has the effect of sharply focusing attention on new developments. No friend to promiscuous sociability, as we know, he comments on the recent increase in Emma's social engagements:

'Increase!'
'Certainly; you must be sensible that the last half year has made a great difference in your way of life.'
'Difference! No indeed I am not.'
'There can be no doubt of your being much more engaged with company than you used to be. Witness this very time. Here am I come down for only one day, and you are engaged with a dinner-party!. . .'

Randalls is responsible for the change, he says, and we recall that his earlier grumblings had been caused by dinner at Randalls on a wintry evening. Mr Weston is incorrigibly addicted to company, by John Knightley's standards; but Randalls now also means Frank Churchill. The two brothers are agreed about Randalls, and we may perhaps be surprised that they do not also specify the

Eltons, knowing that the latter are the reason for the dinner they are now attending. But the Eltons are an incidental menace, Randalls the home of near friends — and of Frank's father. If they see danger for Emma in all this sociability they are right in pointing to Randalls. Mr Weston must be blamed at a later stage (Chapter 42) for the inclusion of the Eltons in the scheme for Box Hill. The 'unmanageable goodwill of Mr Weston's temper' in this situation comes as a surprise to Emma, who supposes that he must be aware of her feelings towards them. The habit of meeting in large parties, in spite of these incompatibilities, continues through to the Box Hill episode, when everything turns bad and the group disintegrates. Until that point friends naturally wish to be with friends. Emma supports the Westons, and Mr Knightley would never be absent from an occasion that concerned Emma. Indeed Emma, as we have seen, has a strong tendency to participate, and to enjoy a social occasion, whatever her initial reservations. But the danger to her is real and in the unnatural atmosphere of Box Hill good manners suddenly collapse.

Of the two characters whose pressure Emma feels most during this phase of the book, Frank Churchill and Mrs Elton, the latter may be viewed in simple terms. Readers from the beginning have greatly relished this portrait, but it may be asked whether Jane Austen overdid it. Was she reverting to the style of those studies in undeviating, unrelenting vulgarity found in Fanny Burney? This would be a defect. But another possibility, which re-readings tend to confirm, is that she has some special animus here, and quite deliberately confronts Emma with this mortal threat to the quality of life at Highbury of which she, Emma, may be an imperfect representative but is a jealous and vigorous custodian. The fact that Mrs Elton has a great social success confirms our feeling that Highbury society is not fastidious, and may strengthen our sympathy for that part of Emma that prefers very few friends and only the best. In the encounters between the two women Emma faces an extraordinary concentration of bad taste, and she acquits herself well:

'. . . Mr Weston seems an excellent creature — quite a first-rate favourite with me already, I assure you. And *she* appears so truly good — there is something so motherly and kind-hearted about her, that it wins upon one directly. She was your

governess, I think?' Emma was almost too much astonished
to answer; but Mrs Elton hardly waited for the affirmative
before she went on.

'Having understood as much, I was rather astonished to find
her so very lady-like! But she is really quite the gentlewoman.'
'Mrs Weston's manners', said Emma, 'were always particularly
good. Their propriety, simplicity and elegance, would make
them the safest model for any young woman.'
'And who do you think came in while we were there?'
Emma was quite at a loss. The tone implied some old acquaintance — and how could she possibly guess?
'Knightley!' continued Mrs Elton; — 'Knightley himself!. . .'

Mrs Elton as a threat can only be fully assessed when we see her
role as more than mere encroachment, and that of Emma not
only in terms of refinement keeping its distance or suffering a
bruising encounter. Emma, after all, is not impeccably refined
herself, and one of the more ominous effects of Mrs Elton's
advent is to provoke her, mentally at least, to vulgar heat. This
happens in Chapter 32 on their second meeting:

> The idea of her being indebted to Mrs Elton for what was
> called an *introduction* — of her going into public under the
> auspices of a friend of Mrs Elton's, probably some vulgar,
> dashing widow, who, with the help of a boarder, just made a
> shift to live! — The dignity of Miss Woodhouse, of Hartfield,
> was sunk indeed!

In challenging Emma's position in Highbury society, and so
boldly usurping initiative in schemes of social entertainment, Mrs
Elton confuses Emma and distorts her way of life.

So much for Emma's more general problem, the question of
what company to keep in a community that offers sociability in
various forms, and also the question of her duties to certain
people. *Emma* cannot be numbered among the 'conduct book'
novels, of which *Evelina* is an illustrious example, and clearly-
defined conclusive moral points would be difficult to extract
from most of these episodes. But the theme of the young woman
and how she should behave, and of how she must come to terms
with her society, is continually present, and during this phase of
increasing sociability we, along with Mr Knightley, note the way

several pressures are at work to bring about finally the disaster at Box Hill. Turning to the role of Frank Churchill we must now take into account the intrigue, the secret engagement with Jane, which gives to this sequence of episodes special elements of drama and hidden meaning, and adds to Emma's problems and temptations. Frank does not realise how completely he has deceived Emma, and at the end of his first visit (Chapter 30) he hints to her that perhaps she has suspicions of the truth. He would perhaps have confessed had she not misinterpreted the word 'suspicions' as relating to his feelings towards herself; so the misunderstanding continues to the end. Here Jane Austen shows notable originality in her handling of Emma's emotional response to Frank. A heroine who can watch the progress of her emotions as she declines from the state of being in love (as she thinks) to that of knowing she is not, and can even watch herself with amusement as she fantasises, is a splendid contribution to the development of modern fiction. She has reached this position by the beginning of Chapter 31:

> . . . She was very often thinking of him, and quite impatient for a letter, that she might know how he was, how were his spirits, how was his aunt, and what was the chance of his coming to Randall again this spring. But, on the other hand, she could not admit herself to be unhappy, nor, after the first morning, to be less disposed for employment than usual; she was still busy and cheerful; and, pleasing as he was, she could yet imagine him to have faults; and farther, though thinking of him so much, and, as she sat drawing or working, forming a thousand amusing schemes for the progress and close of their attachment, fancying interesting dialogues, and inventing elegant letters; the conclusion of every imaginary declaration on his side was that she *refused* him. Their affection was always to subside into friendship. Every thing tender and charming was to mark their parting; but still they were to part. . .
> 'I do not find myself making any use of the word *sacrifice*', said she — 'In not one of all my clever replies, my delicate negatives, is there any allusion to making a sacrifice. I do suspect that he is not really necessary to my happiness. . .'

Here indeed we can have hopes for Emma. Misreader of

appearances as she inveterately is, she remains rational about herself, and does not take herself too seriously. This makes it easier for us to entertain the very sympathetic interpretation of Frank Churchill's 'game' taken by Robert Liddell, who writes very well on the intrigue part of the plot. According to Liddell, Frank thinks that Emma has guessed the secret at a very early stage, and that in the passage where she and Mrs Weston find him alone with Jane, mending Mrs Bates's glasses, the talk that follows concerning the piano and its sender need not be regarded as wantonly mystifying.[3] Frank's speech about the 'true affection' that prompted the gift, followed by Jane's 'smile of secret delight' could be accepted not only as quite moving evidence of the feeling between them, but also as something that Emma is intended to understand as a friend. But she understands nothing. When he comes back from Enscombe for a brief two hour visit, in Chapter 37, she sees signs of agitation in him: 'Lively as he was, it seemed a liveliness that did not satisfy himself. . .' He stays only a quarter of an hour, and we are not told which 'old acquaintances' in Highbury he then calls on. To Emma this simply means that he is no longer in love with herself. Considerable skill goes into the playing down of Frank's attentions to Jane at the ball in Chapter 38. On their arrival Emma notices that he is restless and that he is looking about and 'watching for the sound of other carriages', but a show of interest in Mrs Elton, followed by an introduction to her, somehow covers up the more important fact that the Eltons, by mistake, have failed to bring Jane and Miss Bates. The mistake is rectified, and on the return of the carriage Frank, at the mention of rain, goes off for umbrellas: 'Miss Bates must not be forgotten.' Miss Bates herself, in the comprehensive monologue that soon follows, has much to say about Frank's courtesy to herself and Jane; and to Miss Bates we owe the pleasant picture somewhat later of his renewed attention to both of them: 'I am not helpless. Sir, you are most kind. Upon my word, Jane on one arm and me on the other!' We pay a penalty if we do not note such precious details in her rambling discourse. Without these small pieces of evidence, easily missed — Emma does not notice them — one might conclude that the whole evening goes by without a sign of their acquaintance with each

[3]   But Frank's letter in Chapter 50 gives no specific support here.

other. Everything, in fact, is done to ensure that Emma continues to be deceived. For example, Harriet's adventure with the gypsies, and her misleading conversation with Emma after Frank's intervention, creates a diversion which makes Emma proof against Mr Knightley's warnings at the end of Chapter 41.

If we, on a first reading, are as much deceived as she, not much is lost, because the dominant interest lies in her response to Frank's behaviour, rather than in Frank's reasons. Emma is central, in the foreground, and what we see of her will not change in any way when re-reading and closer inspection tells us more of Frank and Jane. But from Chapter 42 onwards their situation becomes more painful, and though Emma still remains deceived she sees more open signs of trouble. Her cool, humorous reception of him when he arrives late at Donwell Abbey, makes a good scene of comedy which will not look different, so far as her role is concerned, when the whole truth becomes known, but will look very different in the part that concerns Frank. Emma sees that Frank is out of humour: 'Some people were always cross when they were hot. . .eating and drinking were often the cure. . .', and she points the way to the dining-room, in which he professes no interest but to which on second thoughts he has recourse. Later, after he comes back, with his manners somewhat adjusted, presumably after a good meal, the note of discontent and self-pity still remaining in his talk, and his yearnings for travel in 'Swisserland', prompt her again to a practical suggestion:

> 'You are not quite so miserable, though, as when you first came. Go and eat and drink a little more, and you will do very well. Another slice of cold meat, another draught of Madeira and water, will make you nearly on a par with the rest of us.'

A smart exchange follows, in which she suggests that he should come with them to Box Hill the next day. ('It is not Swisserland, but it will be something for a young man so much in want of a change.') And after some slightly childish talk about his being 'cross' if he comes, crosser if he doesn't, which she parries neatly, he eventually agrees to come. Emma does not realise that the young man to whom she has recommended the saving properties of food and drink has just had a most serious quarrel with his *fiancée*. And without this clue we may be unable to read Frank Churchill's behaviour at Box Hill, though we do not need it to

36

appreciate Emma's. Frank begins by being dull, 'silent and stupid'. From the beginning there has been 'a languor, a want of spirits', a tendency to split up into groups, which might be partly due to Frank's lack of animation, partly to his need to be separated from Jane, partly because Frank and Mr Knightley are unlikely to be in the same group, or Emma and Miss Bates, or Emma and the Eltons. One strained relationship could have the effect of accentuating the slighter antipathies of the others. But in this remarkable chapter Jane Austen manages to convey the impression that social occasions, like people, can be freakish. This social occasion behaves in a totally individual way, and is as far removed as possible from these organised parties in Fanny Burney's novels (to Vauxhall, for example) where things take an exemplary course, with just those alarms and embarrassments that such an event might be expected to provide. Frank himself behaves freakishly. After being dull he changes his tone, becomes 'talkative and gay', and begins to flirt with Emma. What happens to Emma is of crucial importance, because this culminating episode which brings all their forced sociability to an end is the one in which, also rather freakishly, she misbehaves. So far as the flirting goes she knows perfectly well what she is doing. It means nothing, but she enjoys it; or, rather, she makes the best of it:

. . .Not that Emma was gay and thoughtless from any real felicity; it was rather because she felt less happy than she had expected. She laughed because she was disappointed. . .

Frank's delight in play which, on Liddell's reading, makes him rather an attractive figure in earlier episodes, now becomes excessive and wilful, and he implicates Emma in silly games to rouse the others from their torpor. His flushed condition, infecting Emma, causes her to commit her tell-tale error at the expense of Miss Bates. Unpardonable as it is, her witticism expresses the impatience that she feels all the time when Miss Bates speaks, and from which she has no doubt suffered during the whole of this period of increased social activity since Jane's arrival. Her wit loses its curb, in response to Frank's, which later becomes even more strident. Meanwhile the party has been breaking up. Mrs Elton has been offended by Emma's behaviour, and the Eltons, rather unpleasantly, dissociate themselves from the scene. The situation between Frank and Jane reaches its veiled culmination, and then Jane and Mrs Bates follow the Eltons. 'Such a scheme,' — these are Emma's sentiments — 'composed of so many ill-assorted people, she hoped never to be betrayed into again.' The word 'betrayed' is significant. Frank has betrayed her, though she cannot know this, by drawing her into complicity with him in an exhibition of provocative flirtation, to wound Jane, and by thrusting upon her the leading role in the party games. But as for 'ill-assorted people', she has been involved with them for some time, through the pressure or initiative of others; and she has survived, until this occasion. Her good nature and sanguine temperament have enabled her, as before, to accept and enjoy what others have arranged, in spite of whatever reservations she may originally have had; but her very readiness to go along with things, to try to make the party go, causes her to be unguarded.

Emma regrets the Box Hill project, but only when Mr Knightley speaks to her does she recognise the full measure of the injury done to Miss Bates. With this rebuke every other preoccupation ceases, and she has one thought only: grief at the wrong she has done, and at her self-exposure to the disapprobation of Mr Knightley. Her tears at the end of the chapter bring to an end a chapter in her life, and this coincides with the termination of a phase in the life of Highbury. With the next chapter there really is a turning over of a new leaf for her. It is characteristic of Jane Austen's mild and humane plotting that Emma's visit of atonement to Miss Bates should bring immediate recognition from Mr Knightley, and reconciliation between them. Another novelist might have heightened Emma's crisis over Mr Knightley by leaving this issue unsettled when the next blow strikes Emma in Chapter 47.

In some respects the most pleasing example of plotting in the whole novel is found in the pair of chapters which bring this brilliant sequence to an end; that is, Chapters 46 and 47. But there will be occasion to dwell upon them in the next part of this essay.

One final point may be made concerning the action of *Emma*. Grounded though it is in events of the characters' social and everyday existence, the tone of which pervades the novel, it contains an extraordinary number of situations involving misunderstandings such as one would associate with an older, more artificial fiction. Mr Elton's feelings relating to Harriet; Emma's relating to Frank; Frank's relating to Emma and to Harriet; Mr Knightley's relating to Jane and to Harriet: all become in their turn a matter for mistaken assumptions or conjectures, and cause complications and further errors in scene after scene. This use of multiple misunderstanding is one of the peculiarities of the book, and the main reason for its being much more intricate than Jane Austen's other works. Jane Austen was extremely well equipped to handle a plot of this kind; but she could use it in the interest of something much more important – character, and situation that illuminates character. It would be untrue then to say that she departed entirely from the older methods of plotting. She used them with great skill, but she subordinated them to purposes which one does not associate primarily with ingenuity and artifice: so much so that, as we have seen, some intelligent, but not very observant, readers had the impression that the book lacked plot.

CHARACTER

(1)

If part of Scott's originality consists in his recognition of communities in the process of historic change, it might be said also of Jane Austen that in *Mansfield Park* and *Emma* the community has a character and may change its character; though the reason for the change lies not in the larger political movements of history which can alter, for example, the relations between the Master of Ravenswood and the people of the locality (in *The Bride of Lammermoor*) but perhaps in the arrivals of new individuals whose way of life can alter that of the group and therefore that of other individuals. In eighteenth century fiction communities lack organic life and have no history, either on the larger or the smaller scale. The juxtaposition of Mr Allworthy and Mr Western is a rhetorical more than a social fact, and we do not think of the joining of the two estates with the marriage of Tom and Sophia as an event in the development of the community. Highbury, on the other hand, is a community that can suffer crucial changes through such events as marriages, and, though it would not have occurred to Jane Austen to emphasise the fact, the marriage of Emma and Mr Knightley, with the other marriages, at the end of the book does make for stabilisation after much hectic activity and unrest.

Characters in *Emma* belong to their community, playing a changing role in it and making a changing impression on it as the narrative proceeds. We are accustomed to something like this in later fiction. For example, Nostromo, in Conrad's novel, is a man with a role in a community extremely susceptible to change, and we see how drastically his role too changes. Similar comments could be made on the leading characters, such as Fielding, in *A Passage to India*. Or, to take an illustration uncoloured by politics, the characters in *To the Lighthouse* exist essentially as members of a group, whether they respond to other members or feel themselves to be apart from them. Growth in some characters and the removal by death of others have changed the pattern of relationships in the community when it assembles again after a ten year interval. A certain episode in the final section may be seen as a growing point in the relationship between James Ramsey and his father. The relation between the development of Emma's behaviour and changes in the way of life of Highbury have already been observed.

Some characters are, in a sense, the creation of their community. Their role may be partly bestowed upon them by others, as with Nostromo, and the instability of such situations is part of the history of communities and their members. The first character to be considered here, Mr Elton, is presented initially in terms of his role as a young unmarried clergyman in a community ready to think well of him. He has been in the nighbourhood for a year and his reputation seems to be very sound, though we never learn what Mr Knightley means when he says: 'Elton is a very good sort of man, and a very respectable vicar of Highbury.' (Chapter 8.) Jane Austen does not treat the subject of religion. We may be disinclined to associate Mr Knightley with polite meaningless words on such matters, but on the other hand he is usually slow to express criticisms of other people, except when the offender is Frank Churchill, or Emma. Presumably Mr Elton satisfies some contemporary standard of adequacy as a clergyman, but in Jane Austen's day as in other periods there were different opinions concerning the appropriate standard. Jane Austen gives us no help. In treating him simply as a social being she certainly intends no irony, but the omission of almost all facts relating to his calling has its effect on the economy of the portrait. If it makes him seem rather a lightweight there is something in the style of presentation that suggests that no serious injustice is being done.

In addition to his general role as an esteemed young clergyman he is cast for another by Emma. She had begun to think of him in connection with match making from the day of the Weston marriage:

> 'Poor Mr Elton! You like Mr Elton, papa, – I must look about for a wife for him. There is nobody in Highbury who deserves him. . .I think very well of Mr Elton. . .'

In her celebrated discourse with Harriet, in Chapter 4, on the importance of good manners in a man, Mr Elton's manners are described as 'superior to Mr Knightley's or Mr Weston's'. He could be safely taken as a model; he is 'good humoured, cheerful, obliging, and gentle'. This is an interesting passage, because we know that Emma greatly prefers the two other gentlemen; but she says that their manners have that element of personal idiosyncrasy which would make it unsafe to model oneself on them. The reader may see something slightly suspect in manners so exemplary; and, of course, what Emma has missed is the fact that they are intended for her special benefit. But this is not all. The chapter ends with a surprise stroke:

> And he was really a very pleasing young man, a young man whom any woman not fastidious might like. He was reckoned very handsome; his person much admired in general, but not by her, there being a want of elegance of feature which she could not dispense with.

In Chapter 6, where we first see Mr Elton in action, full of complaisance and flattery, Emma, though smiling at his 'Exactly so!' nevertheless finds him 'an excellent young man'. We now realise with what mental reservations she can use such expressions. Without actually comparing herself with Harriet she is, in fact, thinking on two planes, and Mr Elton will do very well on one of them. At the end of Chapter 9, again amused by his behaviour as a lover ('there was a sort of parade in his speeches. . .'), she again recognises his 'good and agreeable qualities'. Both are deluded, and from her misinterpretation of his misinterpretation of her an entertaining impression of Mr Elton emerges. Clearly Mr Elton is in a state of great elation at the progress he thinks he is making with Emma, and this expresses itself in unflagging attentiveness. We see him from a rather different angle in John Knightley's witty comment on him:

> '. . .With men he can be rational and unaffected, but when he has ladies to please every feature works.' (Chapter 14.)

The side of him that earns the compliment in the first part of the sentence is not represented in the scenes of which we have evidence. He is exposed mainly in his relations with the ladies.

The turning point in this comedy comes when he fails unaccountably to live up to his role. He responds with alacrity to the invitation to Randalls, notwithstanding Harriet's illness, and there is a piquancy in the image of almost gross happiness that he presents to the bewildered Emma. The symptoms of pleasure — and we know what his expectations ˙are — are monstrously heightened for her:

> It was a done thing; Mr Elton was to go, and never had his broad handsome face expressed more pleasure than at this moment; never had his smile been stronger, nor his eyes more exulting than when he next looked at her. (Chapter 13.)

When she receives the warning that she is herself the target of his attentions, the disconcerting idea penetrates only to the extent that she thinks he has become fickle. At the prospect of a coach ride with him (one remembers here, and Jane Austen must also have remembered, the distressing coachrides of eighteenth century fiction — Evelina with Sir Clement, to say nothing of Harriet Byron and her kidnapper) her fears take only the most trivial form. He has been 'drinking too much of Mr Weston's good wine, and [she] felt sure that he would want to be talking nonsense'. Totally deceived and a little drunk he does indeed make himself splendidly ridiculous, but as the scene develops it becomes for Emma the revelation also of her own disastrous mistakes.

One of her mistakes has been her false assessment of Mr Elton's social qualities. In Chapter 16, where she reflects on the sorry past, she recalls that she had found him 'unnecessarily gallant', but had dismissed this as 'a mere error of judgment, of knowledge, of taste, as one proof among others that he had not always lived in the best society. . .'. And this is the same person whose manners were, at one stage, to be recommended as a model, superior in that respect to those of Mr Knightley and Mr Weston. How are we to take this inconsistency? The likelihood is that Mr Elton, anxious to please Emma, did at first achieve a very competent imitation of the best manners. In this somewhat fluid society, which continually admits people of imperfect gentility, the aspiring newcomer might strive to observe the arts of pleasing more than the established members. And perhaps Mr Elton, gratified with his reception, began soon to overdo it. But there is also the possibility that Emma, from the beginning, was unconsciously adjusting her estimate of Mr Elton to a standard relevant to Harriet. Only at a certain level of society, after all, does one need to think of a 'model' of behaviour. At Mr Knightley's level a gentleman needs only to be himself.

For several chapters he disappears from the story, and then re-appears with his dreadful wife, whose every aspect reflects discredit on him and reinforces sharply Emma's view that he has not always been in the best society. For a moment, in Chapter 32, the comedy of the early sequence is recalled when Emma realises that Mr Elton has the peculiar ill-luck of 'being in the same room with the woman he has just married, the woman he wanted to marry, and the woman he had been expected to marry.' During the next sequence of chapters Mrs Elton attracts a degree of social attention that leaves him rather eclipsed. But he occupies the centre again in the very remarkable scene at the ball when he refuses to dance with Harriet. The revelation is sudden and complete, and Mr Elton sinks to a very low level in the human scale:

. . .But Emma's wonder lessened soon afterwards, on seeing Mr Elton sauntering about. He would not ask Harriet to dance if it were possible to be avoided: she was sure he would not — and she was expecting him every moment to escape into the card-room.

Escape, however, was not his plan. He came to the part of the room where the sitters-by were collected, spoke to some, and walked about in front of them, as if to show his liberty, and his resolution of maintaining it. He did not omit being sometimes before Miss Smith, or speaking to those who were close to her. — Emma saw it. She was not yet dancing; she was working her way up from the bottom, and had leisure there-fore to look around, and by only turning her head a little she saw it all. When she was half way up the set, the whole group were exactly behind her, and she would no longer allow her eyes to watch; but Mr Elton was so near, that she heard every syllable of a dialogue which just then took place between him and Mrs Weston; and she perceived that his wife, who was standing immediately above her, was not only listening also, but even encouraging him by significant glances. — The kind-hearted, gentle Mrs Weston had left her seat to join him and say, 'Do not you dance, Mr Elton?' to which his prompt reply was, 'Most readily, Mrs Weston, if you will dance with me.'

'Me! — oh! no — I would get you a better partner than my-self. I am no dancer.

'If Mrs Gilbert wishes to dance,' said he. 'I shall have great pleasure, I am sure — for, though beginning to feel myself rather an old married man, and that my dancing days are over, it would give me very great pleasure at any time to stand up with an old friend like Mrs Gilbert.'

'Mrs Gilbert does not mean to dance, but there is a young lady disengaged whom I should be very glad to see dancing — Miss Smith.' 'Miss Smith! — oh! — I had not observed. — You are extremely obliging — and if I were not an old married man. — But my dancing days are over, Mrs Weston. You will excuse me. Any thing else I should be most happy to do, at your command —, but my dancing days are over.'

Mrs Weston said no more; and Emma could imagine with what surprise and mortification she must be returning to her seat. This was Mr Elton! the amiable, obliging, gentle Mr Elton. — She looked round for a moment; he had joined Mr Knightley at a little distance, and was arranging himself for settled conversation, while smiles of high glee passed between him and his wife.

She would not look again. Her heart was in a glow, and she feared her face might be as hot.

In another moment a happier sight caught her; — Mr Knightley leading Harriet to the set!. . . (Chapter 38.)

'Evil' is a word much cheapened in contemporary literary discussion, but the image of Mr Elton 'sauntering' (seeking whom he may devour), is truly hideous. What he does to Harriet is entirely deliberate, and his disgusting pleasure in no way concealed. Evil on a lilliputian scale, naturally: that would be Mr Elton's measure. But in its small way it is complete and unmistakeable.

Jane Austen handles the immediate aftermath with great economy. No sooner does Mr Elton join Mr Knightley than the latter abandons him and turns to Harriet. The rescue of Harriet is the important thing; the cutting of Mr Elton, with whatever Mr Knightley may have been thinking, can be left to be understood. A few lines later, Mr Elton, 'looking very foolish', makes for the card room. Economy marks her treatment of the entire episode. Virtually over in one page, with all that it tells us, it is hardly referred to again and it seems to make no difference to the social relationships of the circle. Whether or not Mr Weston knows all that his wife witnessed at the ball the Eltons are included in his social schemes. Whatever Mr Knightley thinks of Mr Elton he says little, and participates on all the occasions when he and his wife, and Emma, are present. The novelist is equally reticent. Hardly anything is made of the fact that, at the end of the book, when weddings take place, the marriage service is read and a blessing invoked by Mr Elton. Another novelist might have been tempted to dwell on such an incongruity. The plainness of Jane Austen's treatment, her abstention from any exploitation of piquancies, expresses perhaps her straightforward recognition of the *ordinariness* of this state of affairs. In societies, especially small ones, where people are cohesively linked together a piece of mean behaviour on the part of one of them may be lived down, and people have to be lived with in spite of faults. Tolerance will be the greater if the offender is a clergyman, because a clergyman is nothing if not central in such communities.

To sum up: Mr Elton may be regarded as a comic character, but not with the finality that would exclude him from another, more unpleasant category. He is cast at first in a comic role, but when that ceases he takes on others. Apparently he can also play a straight role, that of the 'respectable' vicar. This is an example of mature characterisation on Jane Austen's part, and an important feature of it is the avoidance of the fixed category such as the term 'comic character' denotes. This category belongs to traditional literary artifice, and Jane Austen did more perhaps than any other writer to transcend it.

(2)

A similar point may be made about the treatment of a much pleasanter character, Mr Weston. The novel begins with his marriage to Emma's former governess and friend, Miss Taylor. He is described, in the novelist's words, in Chapter 1 as 'a man of unexceptionable character, easy fortune, suitable age and pleasant manners,' and from the outset we know him to be respected by the best of judges, Mr Knightley. Speaking of Emma's claim that she played a crucial role as matchmaker, Mr Knightley says: 'A straightforward, open-hearted man, like Weston, and a rational, unaffected woman, like Miss Taylor, may be safely left to manage their own business.' All Miss Taylor's friends, he says, are glad to see her so happily married. But in the brief sketch of his early career in the next chapter there are discreet indications of another view of Mr Weston. When the offer came from the Churchills to adopt his son Frank, 'some scruples and some reluctance', it is suggested, 'the widower-father may be supposed to have felt. . .', but they were overcome, and consequently, 'he had only his own comfort to seek, and his own situation to improve as he could.'. And what with an opportunity in trade created by his brothers, 'a concern which brought just employment enough,' and 'the pleasures of society' at Highbury, 'the next eighteen or twenty years of his life passed cheerfully away.'. His second marriage, we are assured, promised him greater happiness than he has ever had before, but 'he had never been an unhappy man.' Jane Austen does not press hard, but the transaction that was to decide Frank's future fortunes and, in some measure, form his character, cannot be viewed as unimportant. She emphasises Mr Weston's cheerful way of life rather than any implication that he may have paid too high a price for ease; but expressions like 'he had never been an unhappy man' may now be seen as having a slight humorous nuance. The fact that Frank, who has never been to Highbury — Mrs Churchill is possessive and demanding — fails to pay a visit after his father's second marriage disturbs Mr Weston much less than his wife. Mrs Weston is exceedingly disappointed when the letter arrives cancelling the visit, and Mr Weston 'for half an hour. . .was surprised and sorry; but he then began to perceive that Frank's coming two or three months later would be a much better plan; better time of year; better weather', and so on. Perhaps he is covering up a little, and it is on his behalf as much as her own that Mrs Weston is upset; but, on the other hand, his easy acceptance of his son's behaviour tallies only too well with what we know of his character. The love of ease would seem to be hereditary, and in Frank it takes an especially dubious form; but Jane Austen does not say this, and we must be careful not to force the emphasis. No open reflection on Mr Weston occurs in this chapter.

The first criticism of him on Emma's part appears in Chapter 38. The evening of the ball at the Crown has arrived, and Mr

Weston has asked Emma to come early, 'for the purpose of taking her opinion as to the propriety and comfort of the rooms before any other persons come.' But when she is there she witnesses the arrival of another carriage containing, as she discovers, 'a family of old friends', who were coming like herself, 'by particular desire, to help Mr Weston's judgment; and they were so very closely followed by another carriage of cousins, who had been entreated to come early with the same distinguishing earnestness, on the same errand, that it seemed as if half the company might soon be collected together for the purpose of preparatory inspection':

> Emma perceived that her taste was not the only taste on which Mr Weston depended, and felt, that to be the favourite and intimate of a man who had so many intimates and confidantes, was not the very first distinction in the scale of vanity.

This is farce, but the situation occupies a subsidiary place in a sequence of events leading to more important matters, and the absurdity is not much exploited. Critics of *Emma* seldom allude to it. Mr Weston is seen here as a comic character, but again, as in the case of Mr Elton, not quite in the usual sense implied in that phrase. Comic characters, in the tradition that produced Zeal-in-the-Land Busy, Mrs Slipslop, Squire Western, Commodore Trunnion, and Mrs Gamp, have their own style which differentiates them from 'serious' characters. There is a heightened colouring, a special speech idiom; and comedy demands a limitation of their possibilities, so that, except in complex cases such as that of Falstaff, they are not associated with distress and death. They tend to be comic also in their virtues and in their happiness. Parson Adams, the soul of goodness, is good within a comic framework. In the variegated fiction of the period before Jane Austen – and in writers like Dickens after her time – certain adjustments may be needed when comic characters have dealings with non-comic characters, and this may impose some limitation on the latter. In fact a serious character cannot be developed far in the direction of reality, and also maintain a relationship with a character fashioned in the comic style. The formalised gravity of Mr Allworthy's speech is as much a matter of literary artifice as the West country foxhunting rhetoric of Mr Western, so the two characters can be brought together in some kind of verbal dialectic. In the novels of Dickens a strong element of sentiment or romance in the other characters often makes it possible for them to accommodate the great comic. But the society of Jane Austen's Highbury, rooted as it is in the everyday, judges people by the standards that govern everyday behaviour, and all the characters are in the same style, more or less.

In such a world, as in the real one, people may be comic, but not in a way that places them and fixes them in a special category. The manifestations of absurdity in Mr Weston at the beginning of Chapter 38 are almost of the kind that could have earned him a place in that category; but Jane Austen controls the effect, and deflects our attention in the direction of Emma's foibles. In her confident criticism of Mr Weston at this point she also becomes slightly comic, and we learn more about her than about him:

> She liked his open manners, but a little less of open-hearted-ness would have made him a higher character. – General benevolence, but not general friendship, made a man what he ought to be.

Mr Weston has his finest hour in one of the great sequences of the novel: the series of episodes occupying Chapter 46 and 47, which were mentioned but not examined in the previous chapter. In these chapters three important revelations follow in a beautifully planned succession and the novel reaches an unexpected climax. Chapter 46 begins with Mr Weston's arrival at Hartfield, in a splendid state of agitation, with the request that Emma should step over with him as soon as possible to Randalls, to hear something from Mrs Weston:

> 'Depend upon me – but ask me no questions. You will hear it all in time. The most unaccountable business. But hush! hush!'

In response to Emma's pleas for information he tells her that his wife will 'break it to her' better than he can, as if the word 'break' is likely to reduce her alarm. Assured that illness in her sister's family is not the reason for his hurried visit, she now wonders whether Frank Churchill's prospects have been dashed by the sudden emergence of 'half a dozen natural children' in the Churchill family. Mr Weston's confusion could not be bettered. He cannot remember what he has said to Emma, and is ridicu-lously at a loss when he inadvertently mentions Frank's name:

'Who is that gentleman on horseback?' said she, as they proceeded — speaking more to assist Mr Weston in keeping his secret, than with any other view.

'I do not know. — One of the Otways. — Not Frank; — it is not Frank, I assure you. You will not see him. He is half way to Windsor by this time.'

'Has he been with you, then?

'Oh! yes — did you not know? — Well, well, never mind.' For a moment he was silent; and then added, in a tone much more guarded and demure,

'Yes, Frank came over this morning, just to ask us how we did.'

Emma will immediately learn that Frank came over for a very different reason. In their private conversation she is able to tell Mrs Weston that the great news, of Frank's long concealed engagement to Jane Fairfax, does not touch her emotionally. In spite of Frank's misdemeanour, about which Emma really feels very strongly, the two women decide to adopt a tone of ease, and even of congratulation, when Mr Weston re-appears. He is nervous, and needs a look from his wife to convince him that all is well, but 'its happy effect on his spirits was immediate. His air and voice recovered their usual briskness. . .' By the end of the chapter he is 'not far from thinking it [the engagement] the very best thing that Frank could possibly have done.'

With the next chapter comes a change of theme. Emma must once again experience anxiety about Harriet who, or so she believes, has been cherishing hopes of Frank. Mr Weston has emphasised most explicitly the need for keeping the engagement secret, but an exception, she feels, must be made for Harriet. And now Harriet's footsteps and voice are audible, so her problem — would it were as easy as Mrs Weston's — must be faced without delay:

'Well, Miss Woodhouse!' cried Harriet, coming eagerly into the room — is not this the oddest news that ever was?'

Mr Weston has told Harriet, but with the stipulation, of course, that 'it was to be a great secret.' The momentary touch of comedy is forgotten as the chapter moves to its superb culmination. Harriet's indifference to Frank Churchill brings on the all-important confession that not he but Mr Knightley has occupied her thoughts, and now Emma suffers the shock of her life and the supreme test of her self-control as she listens to the tale of Harriet's hopes. But in the chapter that follows she finds amusement again in Mr Weston's inability to keep secrets:

'Such things,' he observed [referring to the engagement] 'always get about.' Emma smiled, and felt that Mr Weston had very good reason for saying so.

Mr Weston's reception of the news of Emma's forthcoming marriage (Chapter 53) is entirely in character. His surprise lasts no longer than five minutes, and soon he almost believes that he had foreseen it from the start. Convinced of the need to keep it secret he tells it to a sufficient number of people to ensure that it will reach everybody. We read that 'the principals', meaning Mr Knightley and Emma, knew what to expect. But it must be stressed again that neither here nor at any other point in the book does Mr Knightley pass remarks on Mr Weston's comic idio-syncrasies. As we have seen (Chapter 36) Mr Knightley and his brother both see Randalls as the cause of Emma's increasing social involvement, and at an earlier point (Chapter 30) Mr Knightley speaks of Mr Weston's readiness to take a lot of trouble for 'a few hours of noisy entertainment', but no suggestion ever appears of his finding Mr Weston funny. Perhaps this is because Mr Weston's general character and manner, at most times, tone in sufficiently with those of his community, or because Mr Knightley is not in the habit of indulging a sense of humour at the expense of people whom he respects. Near the end of the novel, when Mr Knightley expresses indignation at Frank's be-haviour, he notes with displeasure his easy allusion to his father's 'disposition':

'Mr Weston's sanguine temper was a blessing on all his upright and honourable exertions; but Mr Weston earned every present comfort before he endeavoured to gain it.' (Chapter 51.)

If the comic side of Mr Weston provokes little comment within the novel, it is also not referred to often by readers. And, as we have seen, Jane Austen handles it with care, usually subordinating it to matters of more pressing concern.

Comic characters, as we have noted, sometimes have their

special idiom, and there are signs of this in Mr Weston, but not such as would make anyone wish to label him. When Mr Woodhouse cautions Frank against puddles Mr Weston says: 'Frank knows a puddle of water when he sees it, and as to Mrs Bates's, he may get there from the Crown in a hop, step, and jump! (Chapter 23.) Later, at Hartfield (Chapter 35.), he says that his wife is 'as impatient as the black gentleman when any thing is to be done.' These pleasantries set a tone of easy, innocuous undistinguished chat which one readily associates with him.

(3)

The maturity of Jane Austen's characterisation in *Emma* bears a relation, as we have seen, to the fact that the characters belong to a community which can contain them, a tolerably lifelike community with a day to day round of activities, in which each of its members can be seen as participating. Such a community could not absorb a comic character of the old traditional order. But this integrated art will not be found in such completeness in all Jane Austen's novels, and *Pride and Prejudice* is a striking example of something different. Here she comes nearest to the old tradition of the comic character. Mrs Bennet and Mr Collins are perhaps borderline cases. Their community can just contain them, but at a cost. Mrs Bennet's silliness has something of the consistency and relentlessness of silly characters in the comedy of manners, and her unawareness of her effect on others is, like their's, total. The newcomer to Jane Austen delights in Mrs Bennet, that is, in the purely local humour she provides; but with re-readings one must take a harder look at the problem she poses. Even at the end of the book it remains difficult to imagine even the briefest exchange between Mrs Bennet and Mr Darcy. Exchanges between the mother and the second daughter do occur, but some readers may find it hard to believe that Elizabeth must really take the daily brunt. Has too much been sacrificed for the local effect of Mrs Bennet's outbursts? Mr Collins's famous proposal to Elizabeth is excellent comedy, but again of the local kind. In the Bennet household, which includes two unabashed connoisseurs of the absurd, Mr Collins's role is to put on a performance to their taste. In the milieu of Lady Catherine his absurdity and hers keep each other in countenance. Mr Collins has no function apart from his absurdity, which colours all he says and does. But the novelist does try to account for it in terms that relate him to norms, and he is part of the world (though near its periphery) where the norms operate:

> Mr Collins was not a sensible man, and the deficiency of nature had been but little assisted by education or society; the greatest part of his life having been spent under the guidance of an illiterate and miserly father; and though he belonged to one of the universities, he had merely kept the necessary terms, without forming at it any useful acquaintance. The subjection in which his father had brought him up, had given him originally great humility of manner, but it was a good deal counteracted by the self-conceit of a weak head, living in retirement, and the consequential feelings of early and unexpected prosperity. . .(Chapter 15.)

This is a case history, and it explains up to a point why Mr Collins is not as other men. But an air of the impossible, the quintessentially fatuous, hangs about him nevertheless. In a scene like that in Chapter 18, where Elizabeth has the mortifying thought that 'had her family [of which Mr Collins is a member] made an agreement to expose themselves as much as they could during the evening, it would have been impossible for them to play their parts with more spirit, or finer success', Mr Collins's contribution finds its context. He makes egregious speeches to which there can be no reply. Some stare, others smile, and Mr Darcy remains silent. One cannot imagine him in Highbury.

The great popularity of *Pride and Prejudice*, even by comparison with Jane Austen's other books, must be due in some degree to these salient figures. But they stand out in relief to an extent that diminishes relatedness. This rather impoverishes the presentation of the community, and makes the life of the novel as a whole less dense.

Great authors take risks, and Jane Austen's choice of heroines, and of the circumstances threatening them, often shows an artistic courage worthy of her high rank. Elizabeth Bennet, for example, most admirable and most popular of heroines, is nevertheless her father's daughter, with a shade too much fondness for the ridiculous; and her position of social disadvantage presents her with too much occasion for a defiant outspokenness which sometimes approaches the limits of the tolerable. Fanny Price, on the other hand as the youngest, the least assured and the least robust member of the Mansfield Park household, with a conscience as delicate as her constitution, represents a different kind of risk and some readers feel that the dangers of such a choice were not averted. Emma presents almost the exact opposite of Fanny, with faults that continually challenge our tolerance, and Jane Austen is not afraid to show them specifically in operation, with all details. Chapter 7, in which she makes sure of Harriet's rejection of Robert Martin's proposal, putting more pressure than she wishes to admit, makes painful reading; and even after the Elton fiasco she can still act with terrible self-confidence in the equally painful episode (Chapter 23) where she strictly monitors poor Harriet's visit to the Martins, restricting it to its fourteen minutes. Emma feels the suffering that this must cause, but, sure of her rightness, she cannot repent. Lionel Trilling, in the essay quoted earlier, has given an excellent explanation of our sympathetic acceptance of Emma, in spite of her faults. To quote him further:

> We come close to Emma because, in a strange way, she permits us to – by being very close to herself. . . She believes she is clever, she insists that she is right, but she never says that she is good. A consciousness is always at work in her, a sense of what she ought to be and do. It is not an infallible sense, anything but that, yet she does not need us, or the author, or Mr Knightley, to tell her, for example, that she is jealous of Jane Fairfax and acts badly to her. . .

Within this very impressive moral frame, Jane Austen can afford to make Emma in some respects a comic character. In places where a straight account of her attitudes is presented unobtrusive comic inflections are discernible. A good illustration may be found in Chapter 16, which follows upon the episode with Mr Elton in the coach: 'The hair was curled, and the maid sent away, and Emma sat down to think and be miserable. . .' One passage will suffice:

> . . .The distressing explanation she had to make to Harriet, and all that poor Harriet would be suffering, with the awkwardness of future meetings, the difficulties of continuing or discontinuing the acquaintance, of subduing feelings, concealing resentment, and avoiding eclat, were enough to occupy her in most unmirthful reflections some time longer, and she went to bed at last with nothing settled but the conviction of her having blundered most dreadfully.
>
> To youth and natural cheerfulness like Emma's, though under temporary gloom at night, the return of day will hardly fail to bring return of spirits. The youth and cheerfulness of morning are in happy analogy, and of powerful operation; and if the distress be not poignant enough to keep the eyes unclosed, they will be sure to open to sensations of softened pain and brighter hope.
>
> Emma got up on the morrow more disposed for comfort than she had gone to bed, more ready to see alleviations of the evil before her, and to depend on getting tolerably out of it.

Another novelist might have noted more pointedly Emma's capacity to sleep well. The words 'if the distress [it is Harriet's distress] be not poignant enough to keep the eyes unclosed' are somehow slipped in between sentiments so innocent and harmless that they might — indeed, they do — pass unnoticed. The fact is that Emma's good health and resilience are of positive value. No good purpose would have been served by her lying awake half the night, though the decorum of sensibility might prescribe it. Jane Austen neither mocks the decorum of sensibility nor suggests that Emma is too tough. The reader may select this aspect of Emma, her indestructible buoyancy and cheerfulness, as comic, but the novelist has so embedded the comedy in the context that the total statement could appear to read as rather favourable to Emma or, at the most, neutral. Thackeray would have ruined Emma's character for us; even George Eliot would have said too much.

The first paragraph offers a good example of the 'closeness' to Emma of which Trilling writes. It exposes Emma, perhaps, but what does it do to the reader, if he is honest? Emma gets her priorities right: 'all that Harriet would be suffering' comes first. But only a comma separates this from thoughts of social embarrassment, and we see how fertile she is in imagining different kinds of embarrassment, how very readily her mind turns to such themes. Jane Austen gives us no lead here. The sequence is uncoloured by the slightest satirical emphasis. If we wish to accuse Emma of turning too quickly from Harriet's suffering to embarrassments which will also affect herself, the choice lies with us, and we may decide that Jane Austen's knowledge of general human nature here is too true for comfort. We are free to extract the comic point, but at our own risk. It has not been forced upon us. And like so much comedy in real life it can be viewed neutrally even by intelligent people, because not everyone focuses on the comic. Many quite competent readers would take the whole of this passage straight. If Emma could be accused, in this scene, of being excessively tough, a most impressive passage occurs later in the novel where toughness comes into its own. The brilliant sequence, already examined in part, which consists of chapters 46 and 47 and begins with the comedy of Mr Weston's agitation, comes to an extraordinary climax with Emma's sudden moment of self-realisation as she recognises the state of Harriet's hopes. Toughness comes into its own because Emma must now control feelings of surprising intensity. Here again we are very close to Emma as the various ingredients of her mental state are specified. The language may be generalised, as Emma sees how inconsiderate, how indelicate, how irrational and so forth her behaviour has been, and 'what blindness, what madness' has led her on. It is also rather formalised in the eighteenth century way, and this is not amiss. Emma's moral sense, though genuine, would find the conventional, rhetorical terms sufficient. But her plight, as she sits with Harriet, is stated in language that does justice to less ideal factors than conscience and duty:

. . .Some portion of respect for herself, however, in spite of these demerits − some concern for her own appearance, and a strong sense of justice by Harriet − (there would be no need of *compassion* to the girl who believed herself loved by Mr Knightley — but justice required that she should not be made unhappy by any coldness now,) gave Emma the resolution to sit and endure farther with calmness, with even apparent kindness. — For her own advantage indeed, it was fit that the utmost extent of Harriet's hopes should be enquired into; and Harriet had done nothing to forfeit the regard and interest which had been so voluntarily formed and maintained — or to deserve to be slighted by the person, whose counsels had never led her right. — Rousing from reflection, therefore, and subduing her emotion, she turned to Harriet again, and, in a more inviting accent, renewed the conversation; for as to the subject which had first introduced it, the wonderful story of Jane Fairfax, that was quite sunk and lost. — Neither of them thought but of Mr Knightley and themselves.

Harriet, who had been standing in no unhappy reverie, was yet very glad to be called from it, by the now encouraging manner of such a judge, and such a friend as Miss Woodhouse, and only wanted invitation, to give the history of her hopes with great, though trembling delight. — Emma's tremblings as she asked, and as she listened, were better concealed than Harriet's, but they were not less. Her voice was not unsteady; but her mind was in all the perturbation that such a development of self, such a burst of threatening evil, such a confusion of sudden and perplexing emotions, must create. — She listened with much inward suffering, but with great outward patience, to Harriet's detail. — Methodical, or well arranged, or very well delivered, it could not be expected to be; but it contained, when separated from all the feebleness and tautology of the narration, a substance to sink her spirit — especially with the corroborating circumstances, which her own memory brought in favour of Mr Knightley's most improved opinion of Harriet.

Emma's concern for her own self-respect, the no more than 'apparent' kindness with which she endures Harriet's conversation, the development of 'self': all these are symptoms hardly in accordance with the decorum associated with heroines, even after Jane Austen; but they have the effect, not of lessening our admiration for her, but of revealing her moral strengths in their close relation to the primitive forces to which they are allied but which they must hold in check. Possessiveness, sheer will, what Jane Austen calls 'self': these, rather than sex, are the terms in which Emma's nature is here presented, and they are primitive enough. It is especially appropriate that Harriet, during this episode, should appear at her most foolish. She is day-dreaming ('in no unhappy reverie') when Emma invites her to begin. The description of her weaknesses in narration must reflect Emma's irratable state of nerves: an acute piece of psychology. At the very moment when kindness to Harriet is most called for, and most difficult to achieve, her poverty of manner increases the strain. Harriet's misconceptions relating to Mr Knightley are the extreme limit of her departure from reality and common sense, and here we see her as rather spoilt, and capable of rudeness when Robert Martin's name is mentioned.

The goodness of Emma in this chapter may appeal to us all the more for not being an ideal goodness. It only just succeeds. Justice is done to Harriet's story, and with great effort an ugly situation avoided, and that is all. But in Emma's state of raw anguish, with so much of 'self' to contend with, and with what she recognises as her very limited natural supply of tenderness, the achievement must win our respect.

The portrait of Emma is wonderfully rounded. We see her with the novelist's humorous awareness, when Emma is unaware; but, as we have seen, Emma also achieves humorous self-awareness in the place already noted where she imagines her charming refusal of Frank Churchill; and even in one of her worst moments, at Box Hill, she sees herself almost cynically as she supposes others may see her. Frank's gallantry which, in her falsely enlivened state, she encourages, means nothing, as she knows, but

in the judgment of most people looking on it must have had such an appearance as no English word but flirtation could very well describe. 'Mr Frank Churchill and Miss Woodhouse flirted together excessively.' They were laying themselves open to that very phrase – and to having it sent off in a letter to Maple Grove by one lady, to Ireland by another. (Chapter 43.)

It would be a pleasure to be able to say that this art of rounded portraiture was inherited and developed by later English novelists; but it would be only partly true. In Dorothea Brooke we have another case of the heroine who is serious and admirable, but also a little eccentric and capable of absurd error; but humorous self-awareness is hardly in her line. George Eliot is the writer to whom we would naturally look, and she fails us in this respect. As we have already seen, she deals more ambitiously with her heroines, and takes them further on the road of experience, but this does not necessarily lead to greater compositional richness or sharpness in the actual portrayal of character.

Some of the qualities we are especially concerned with here are more likely to recur in American authors, especially Henry James. Americans, with their 'low-keyed humour of defeat', to use Constance Rourke's excellent phrase, are more liable to show a sense of the mixed character of situations. Milly Theale and Maggie Verver have their moments of wry humorous self-awareness, while Strether (to turn away from heroines) has a very keen sense of the incongruities and drolleries of his role, his creator being aware of others. But these characters belong so much to the American tradition that one hesitates to associate them with any specific element contributed by Jane Austen.

Jane Austen's most obvious contribution in her characterisation of Emma, is the conception of a heroine with serious defects. Earlier heroines, like Clarissa, had made tragic errors, but in circumstances of extreme pressure. They do not lose thereby their ideal quality. But Emma's errors are caused by ordinary uncomely faults: lack of consideration for others, a conceited opinion of her own judgment. She is the first of the distinguished line of great faulty heroines in English fiction. Perhaps hers is the best composed portrait of all.

STYLE AND MANNERS

(1)

Much has been said here about the rhetorical aspect of eighteenth century fiction, which at close quarters becomes a matter of literary style. It may be useful here to note a few examples of the difference in prose style between Jane Austen and some of her predecessors. The difference is not total. In some respects her affinity is more with the eighteenth century than with her successors of the Victorian period.

In general, as we have seen, eighteenth century heroines are rhetorically conceived, and this differentiates them from Jane Austen's heroines. Only the merest mention needs to be made of the notorious passage introducing Sophia Western.[1] Amelia's charms inspire a panegyric with supporting quotations from Milton, Waller and Suckling.[2] The description of Emily's perfections in *Peregrine Pickle*[3] actually contains such items as 'her teeth regular and white as driven snow'. Cecilia, in Fanny Burney's novel, is presented in these lofty terms:

> But though thus largely indebted to fortune, to nature she had yet greater obligations: her form was elegant, her heart was liberal; her countenance announced the intelligence of her mind, her complexion varied with every emotion of her soul, and her eyes, the heralds of her speech, now beamed with understanding and now glistened with sensibility.[4]

When she wrote *Emma* Jane Austen had got beyond humorous allusions to earlier novelists, but against this background her simple 'Emma Woodhouse, handsome, clever, and rich' has the effect of a stroke of style.

One of the familiar arts of eighteenth century novelists

[1] *Tom Jones*, Book IV, Ch.2.
[2] *Amelia*, Vol.VI, Ch.1.
[3] Ch.20.
[4] *Cecilia, or Memoirs of an Heiress*, Vol. 1, Ch. 1.

consisted in a distancing of ludicrous or violent events, which can also be seen as a humorous enhancement of them, by the use of certain urbanities of diction which are very far from Jane Austen's style, because her relation to her subject-matter did not require this kind of literary play. The French marquis, at the famous banquet in the ancient style in *Peregrine Pickle*, is 'driven to the extremity of his condescension' by one taste of the soup.[5] 'Not to be outdone in courtesy', Parson Adams retaliates in the tavern brawl.[6] Jane Austen had little occasion for a style that so elaborately embellishes the facts. Yet traces of this style, applied to very different situations, may be found in her work. The following passage, in Chapter 9 of *Emma*, is very interesting in this respect. It occurs at the point in the novel when Emma has done her worst, so far as Robert Martin's courtship is concerned, and Mr Knightley has said what he thinks about it: a point where Emma may be said to have committed herself deeply to a responsibility for Harriet:

> Her views of improving her little friend's mind, by a great deal of useful reading and conversation, had never yet led to more than a few first chapters, and the intention of going on tomorrow. It was much easier to chat than to study; much pleasanter to let her imagination range and work at Harriet's fortune, than to be labouring to enlarge her comprehension or exercise it on sober facts; and the only literary pursuit which engaged Harriet at present, the only mental provision she was making for the evening of life, was the collecting and transcribing all the riddles of every sort that she could meet with, into a thin quarto of hot-pressed paper, made up by her friend, and ornamented with cyphers and trophies.
>
> *In this age of literature*, such collections on a very grand scale are not uncommon. Miss Nash, head-teacher at Mrs Goddard's, had written out at least three hundred; and Harriet, who had taken the first hint of it from her, hoped, with Miss Woodhouse's help, to get a great many more. Emma assisted with her *invention, memory and taste*; and as Harriet wrote a very pretty hand, it was likely to be an arrangement of the first order, in form as well as quantity.

[5] Ch.48.
[6] *Joseph Andrews*, Book II, Ch.5.

Mr Woodhouse was almost as much interested in the business as the girls, and tried very often to recollect something worth their putting in. 'So many clever riddles as there used to be when he was young. . .' [italics mine]

The first sentence and other parts of the passage are plain and direct, with no play of style. There is moral force, and something that suggests the influence of Samuel Johnson, in 'labouring to enlarge her understanding or exercise it on sober facts', which places time-wasting in relation to lost opportunities and serious values. The only 'work' referred to here is that of the imagination, and on material sufficiently plastic. But in general Jane Austen wants to keep the tone light. Tact and a sense of proportion, and a bland irony, modify the presentation. The irony lies in the two italicised phrases, where Jane Austen plays the eighteenth century game. The humorous compliment to Emma's 'invention, memory and taste' reminds us of the serious attention given to the faculties of the mind by eighteenth century thinkers, and there is rhetoric in the impressive triad. This and the amusingly incongruous reference to 'literature' make for an easy adjustment of tone, while leaving the implications sufficiently sharp. There may be a deliberate allusion to the concluding sentence of Gibbon's *Autobiography*: '. . . but I must reluctantly observe that two causes, the abbreviation of life, and the failure of hope, will always tinge with a browner shade the evening of life.'[7] The use of this sober, mellow phrase in relation to the seventeen year old Harriet is in keeping with the general effect of ease. But Jane Austen does not habitually employ such artifices.

Continuity with the eighteenth century can be seen, and has often been noted, in the vocabulary used by Jane Austen for describing people. Certain generalised expressions appear again and again in passages where new characters are introduced. The formal, conventional recurrence of the same words, and the lack of any attempt at detailed individualisation at this stage of their portrayal is in the spirit of Augustan literary manners. A few quotations will suffice to recall the familiar patterns of reference: 'Mr Bingley was good looking and gentlemanlike; he had a pleasant

[7] *Autobiography of Edward Gibbon. As originally edited by Lord Sheffield*, with an Introduction by J.B. Bury. London 1962, p.221.

countenance, and easy, unaffected manners. . .'[8] And from the same novel: '[Mr Wickham's] appearance was greatly in his favour; he had all the best parts of beauty, a fine countenance, a good figure, and a very pleasing address. The introduction was followed up on his side by a happy readiness of conversation – a readiness at the same time perfectly correct and unassuming. . .' (Chapter 15.) 'Colonel Fitzwilliam. . .was about thirty, not handsome, but in person and address most truly the gentleman. . . [He] entered into conversation directly with the readiness and ease of a well-bred man, and talked very pleasantly. (Chapter 30). [Mr Collins] was a tall, heavy looking man of five and twenty. His air was grave and stately and his manners were very formal.' (Chapter 13.) Turning from *Pride and Prejudice* to *Mansfield Park*: 'Her brother [i.e. Henry Crawford] was not handsome; no, when they first saw him he was absolutely plain, black and plain; but still he was the gentleman, with a pleasing address' (Chapter 5.)'[Mr Rushworth] was a heavy young man, with not more than common sense; but as there was nothing disagreeable in his figure or address, the young lady was well pleased with her conquest'. (Chapter 4). Returning to *Pride and Prejudice* we may note in the following passage the familiar terms, the same social virtues, but with another factor: 'Mr Gardiner was a sensible, gentlemanlike man. . .The Netherfield ladies would have had difficulty in believing that a man who lived by trade, and within view of his own warehouses, could have been so well bred and agreeable.' (Chapter 25.) Emma's first impressions of Frank Churchill in Chapter 23 are in precisely the same terms, but with a heightening, a suggestion of quick, animated appraisal on a sudden introduction, after prolonged expectation:

> The Frank Churchill so long talked of, so high in interest, was actually before her – he was presented to her, and she did not think too much had been said in his praise; he was a *very* good looking young man; height, air, address, all were unexceptionable, and his countenance had a great deal of the spirit and liveliness of his father's; he looked quick and sensible. She felt immediately that she would like him; and there was a well-bred ease of manner, and a readiness of talk, which convinced her that he came intending to be acquainted with

[8] *Pride and Prejudice*, Ch. 3.

her, and that acquainted they soon must be.

First impressions are habitually on this level. In so far as good sense and a well-bred ease are the recurring qualities in favourable descriptions one can see why Jane Austen's values are often associated with those of the eighteenth century. Frank Bradbrook, in a full discussion of her antecedents, quotes Lord Chesterfield's observations on 'the art of pleasing':

> . . . a graceful motion, a significant look, a trifling attention, an obliging word dropped *à propos*, air, dress, and a thousand other indefinable things, make that happy and inestimable composition. . .[9]

Here are some aspects which Jane Austen would not have noted. Chesterfield writes as a worldly connoisseur, while her descriptions represent rather the impression of someone (a woman) with sound traditional criteria, who responds naturally and spontaneously. In more than one case these impressions are an insufficient guide. Elizabeth's standards and intelligence are good, but she does not detect the inner nature of Wickham. Willoughby, who plays a treacherous part in *Sense and Sensibility*, is described at the outset as 'a young man of good abilities, quick imagination, lively spirits, and open affectionate manners.' There is too much openness, in fact, but no impression is given of anything worse. Dr Bradbrook[10] quotes Mr Knightley's distinction between the word 'amiable', which the latter associates with 'delicacy towards the feelings of others', and the French 'aimable', which implies merely having 'good manners and being agreeable'. *Mansfield Park* contains a notable paragraph about the Bertram sisters in which surface manners are placed in an ominous moral context:

> The Miss Bertrams were now fully established among the belles of the neighbourhood; and as they joined to beauty and brilliant acquirements, a manner naturally easy, and carefully formed to general civility and obligingness, they possessed its favour as well as its admiration. Their vanity was in such good order, that they seemed to be quite free from it, and gave themselves no airs; while the praises attending such behaviour,

[9] *Letters to his Son*, London, 18 January, O.S. 1750. Quoted in F.W. Bradbrook, *Jane Austen and her Predecessors*, London 1966, p. 31.

[10] *Op. cit.,* p. 32.

secured, and brought round by their aunt, served to strengthen them in believing they had no faults. (Chapter 4.)

This passage takes us beyond first impressions and provides an example of one of Jane Austen's procedures in the presenting of character. Individuals are often seen, as they are here, in relation to the factors contributing to their upbringing. The Bertram sisters have acquired traditional accomplishments (they 'exercise their memories. . .practise their duets'), and certain moral qualities have also been inculcated. Were it nor for Mrs Norris's bad influence — and, of course, Lady Bertram's indolence and Sir Thomas's exacting duties in Parliament — they could be regarded as well brought up. Mr Collins, as we saw earlier, is the product of narrowing influences in early life. But this interest in early influences is shown most frequently in her treatment of women characters. In the very important opening paragraphs of Chapter 42 of *Pride and Prejudice* Elizabeth reflects on the 'impropriety of her father's behaviour as a husband', and on his misuse of talents which might have 'preserved the respectability of his daughters, even if incapable of enlarging the mind of his wife.' The shock of Lydia's elopement is still to come. Perhaps her finest description of an upbringing is the passage in Chapter 20 of *Emma* which describes Jane Fairfax's early life with the Campbells. In words of great beauty Jane Austen brings together the components of a well proportioned, wisely balanced way of life, in which control and order play the most enlightened role:

Such was Jane Fairfax's history. She had fallen into good hands, known nothing but kindness from the Campbells, and been given an excellent education. Living constantly with right-minded and well-informed people, her heart and understanding had received every advantage of discipline and culture; and Col. Campbell's residence being in London, every lighter talent had been done full justice to, by the attendance of first-rate masters. Her disposition and abilities were equally worthy of all that friendship could do; and at eighteen or nineteen she was, as far as such an early age can be qualified for the care of children, fully competent to the office of instruction herself; but she was too much beloved to be parted with. Neither father nor mother could promote, and the daughter could not endure it. The evil day was put off. It was easy to decide that she was still too young; and Jane remained with them, sharing, as another daughter, in all the rational pleasures of an elegant society, and a judicious mixture of home and amusement, with only the drawback of the future, the sobering suggestions of her own good understanding to remind her that all this might soon be over.

Jane's intellectual and artistic accomplishments are well attested, but the secrecy and insecurity of her role in the period covered by the novel prevent her from giving much evidence of the other virtues which such an education seems designed to develop.

It will be noticed that this passage contains a good deal of the verbal balance and antithesis which characterises some eighteenth century prose: '. . .her heart and understanding had received every advantage of discipline and culture.' This suggestion of Augustan eloquence is untypical of Jane Austen. The generalised language, though it might be difficult for us to imagine details which would illustrate the processes referred to, has the wonderful air of being used by someone who knows and has a fine appreciation of these processes. It has often been said that Jane Austen's immediate readers would understand the more detailed application of her vocabulary, and no doubt this was true of some of them. But others would be unreliable judges. Mrs Norris, in a passage which expresses, though not in direct speech, her view of Mrs Rushworth, regards her as 'a pattern of good-breeding and attention', but the novelist, a little earlier (Chapter 8), describes her as a 'well-meaning, civil, prosing, pompous woman'.

Among the key words in Jane Austen's vocabulary 'attention' deserves notice. *Mansfield Park* has many examples of its use. Mr Rushworth in Chapter 9 welcomes the party to Sotherton 'with due attention'. Fanny feels it as a new 'attention' in Chapter 22, when she receives an invitation to dinner from Mrs Grant, and in the next chapter this provokes Mrs Norris to comment on her luck in meeting with 'such attention and indulgence.' In Chapter 25 Fanny's shawl, which Edmund was preparing to put round her shoulders, is seized by Henry Crawford, so that she is 'obliged to be indebted to his more prominent attention.'. Similar uses of the word follow in the next two chapters. Emma, in her chapter of penitence, recognises that her behaviour to Mr Elton had been 'complaisant and obliging. . .full of courtesy and attention'; and in her rejection of Mrs Weston's theory concerning Mr Knightley's attitude to Jane Fairfax, in Chapter 26, she refers to his 'great regard' for the Bateses, his readiness always to 'shew them attention', as a reason for kindnesses which also include Jane. In many cases 'attention' can easily be identified as a specific act, but sometimes its meaning depends on standards of conduct which might vary in accordance with circumstances, or with the sensitiveness of the person in question.

The use of a conventional vocabulary of this kind separates Jane Austen from the early Victorian novelists. The vocabulary dissolves, largely in her own life time, together no doubt with the shared attitudes, and a certain amount of ease is lost. Jane Austen's conservative use of terms did not prevent her from achieving a subtle treatment of character, though the unobtrusiveness of her language may in some places cause the quality of the insight to go unrecognised. Some later writers may go further in the handling of complexities than Jane Austen, but the language of later writers is usually such as to call attention to complexity when it is present.

Perhaps this is the place for a brief mention of Dr Johnson and of Jane Austen's affinity with him. Johnson used a larger and more imposing vocabulary of general terms than his contemporaries, and wielded it with greater moral and intellectual authority. Whether in prose or in verse he could give the most abstract words their full weight of meaning and felt experience. 'Living constantly with right-minded and well-informed people, her heart and understanding had received every advantage of discipline and culture', is precisely the kind of sentence that Johnson's influence at its best might produce. Both writers differ from others of the eighteenth century in the depth at which such meanings were felt by them. Jane Austen was not a Johnson, but Johnson was the only writer who could have set a standard for her.

There are only a certain number of places in *Emma*, which is comedy, after all, where a Johnsonian moral weight would have been appropriate; but one of them is the encounter between Mr Knightley and Emma after Box Hill, followed by Emma's mortification and full recognition (Chapter 44) of the justice of his rebuke:

. . .in her view it was a morning more misspent, more totally bare of rational satisfaction at the time, and more to be abhorred in recollection, than any she had ever passed.

Mr Knightley's appreciation of Miss Bates's case, his detailed and realistic statement of the implications of the sorry incident, are a demonstration of the good sense of which he is the sole representative in the novel. In that phrase 'bare of rational satisfaction' we recognise the marks of the intellectual tradition which is associated with Samual Johnson, but which, in the novel's context, is represented by the influence of Mr Knightley. His influence was exerted in vain in the painful scene (Chapter 8) when Robert Martin and Harriet's prospects provide the theme. Again Mr Knightley's grasp of reality is formidable. All that Emma has been basing her actions on, with regard to Robert Martin, Harriet and Mr Elton, suffers reversal in the light of his clear and detailed appreciation of the facts. This passage has its value in the novel, structurally, as a corrective to the point of view of the heroine, which we have recognised as inadequate but without knowing all that he knows. Mr Knightley's commendation of Robert Martin, composed as it is in the common, generalised idiom, has remarkable impressiveness, because, as in Johnson's moral statements, every word has its full weight:

> . . . Robert Martin's manners have sense, sincerity, and good humour to recommend them; and his mind has more true gentility than Harriet Smith could understand.

Truth such as he can bring to bear on her life finds expression only at these few chosen points in the novel. At the end of this scene Emma is rather demoralised, not penitent, but reduced to a petty, trifling lie about her intentions for Harriet. Mr Knightley gets up in vexation and leaves her. Arnold Kettle pays tribute to another of Mr Knightley's speeches which has this quality. It occurs in Chapter 51, *a propos* of Frank's letter:

> '. . .My Emma, does not everything serve to prove more and more the beauty of truth and sincerity in all our dealings with one another?'

As Professor Kettle says, its force depends 'not on its abstract "correctness" but on the emotional conviction it carries, involving of course our already acquired confidence in Mr Knightley's judgment and character.'.[11] The 'correctness' is in a tradition in which we are accustomed to find this depth of feeling and authority.

Jane Austen's relationship to Johnson must remain elusive because they are very different from each other, and when his qualities reappear in her they are not in the same style nor on the same scale. One of Johnson's gifts was a sardonic recognition of the enormities of the human mind. *The Rambler* abounds in passages such as the following, in No.104, on the desire for flattery:

> . . . We always think ourselves better than we are, and are generally desirous that others should think us still better than we think ourselves. To praise us for actions or dispositions which deserve praise, is not to confer a benefit, but to pay a tribute. We have always pretensions to fame, which, in our own hearts, we know to be disputable, and which we are desirous to strengthen by a new suffrage; we have always hopes which we suspect to be fallacious, and of which we eagerly snatch at every confirmation.[12]

A further example will suffice, an excerpt from an extraordinary paragraph in *Rambler* 111 on the very Johnsonian theme of procrastination:

> At our entrance into the world, when health and vigour give us fair promises of time sufficient for the regular maturation of our schemes, and a long enjoyment of our acquisitions, we are eager to seize the present moment. . . but age seldom fails to change our conduct; we grow negligent of time in proportion as we have less remaining, and suffer the last part of life to steal from us in languid preparations for future undertakings, or slow approaches to remote advantages, in weak hopes of some fortuitous occurrence, or drowsy equilibrations of undetermined counsel. . .[13]

[11] *Introduction to the English Novel*, Vol.1, London 1951, p.93.
[12] Yale edition of *The Works of Samuel Johnson*, Vol.IV. New Haven and London 1969, pp.192-3.
[13] *Op. cit.*, p.227.

Jane Austen would never have written like this. Her descriptions of mental behaviour are verbally more subdued, and sardonic is too strong a word for her wit. But, with due allowance for these differences, we may note a family likeness between passages such as these and some passages in her work. The place in Chapter 16 where Emma, though upset about Harriet, sleeps well and wakes up in a more cheerful frame of mind, has some of the flavour of Johnsonian realism. Johnson is very good on situations where people fail to live up to what tradition expects of them. For example, the hermit in *Rasselas*, far from achieving disciplined contemplation in the desert, finds himself a prey to riotous fantasy, and when the prince and his friends visit him has already decided to return to the city. Perhaps the best example to cite here in Jane Austen is the passage, witty but most endearing, in the last chapter of *Mansfield Park*, depicting the happiness of Fanny:

> My Fanny indeed at this very time, I have the satisfaction of knowing, must have been happy in spite of every thing. She must have been a happy creature in spite of all that she felt or thought she felt, for the distress of those around her. She had sources of delight that must force their way. She was returned to Mansfield Park, she was useful, she was beloved; she was safe from Mr Crawford, and when Sir Thomas came back she had every proof that could be given in his then melancholy state of spirits, of his perfect approbation and increased regard; and happy as all this must have made her, she would still have been happy without any of it, for Edmund was no longer the dupe of Miss Crawford.
>
> It is true that Edmund was very far from happy himself. He was suffering from disappointment and regret, grieving over what was, and wishing for what could never be. She knew it was so, and was sorry; but it was with a sorrow so founded on satisfaction, so tending to ease, and so much in harmony with every dearest sensation, that there are few who might not have been glad to exchange their greatest gaiety for it.

Jane Austen expresses sincere satisfaction at Fanny's state of mind. The reader can share it, and at the same time enjoy phrases like 'in spite of all that she felt or thought that she felt', and 'a sorrow so founded on satisfaction, so tending to ease.'. There was no novelist of the eighteenth century, and no other writer but Johnson, who could have helped to develop in Jane Austen this combination of wit and moral realism in descriptions of states of mind.

On writers of less originality and power than Jane Austen the influence of Johnson could be unfortunate. Fanny Burney in *Cecilia* produced many passages like the following, in the style sometimes labelled Johnsonese. It appears in Chapter 2 and refers to Mr Monckton's career at the Temple:

> . . . But here, too volatile for serious study, and too gay for laborious application, he made little progress: and the same quickness of parts and vigour of imagination which, united with prudence or accompanied by judgment, might have raised him to the head of his profession, being unhappily associated with fickleness and caprice, served only to impede his improvement, and obstruct his preferment.[14]

Here are antithetical patterns of words with insufficient justification in the intellectual content. Jane Austen does not often use antithetical structures, but when she does, as in the paragraph about Jane Fairfax's education, we are made conscious of a meaningful structure of related values, which gives the verbal sequence great felicity.

It may be claimed that these qualities of moral realism and wit, the qualities in which Johnson's influence is most evident, are among those which have most relevance to Jane Austen's contribution to the English novel in the nineteenth century, and to her role in what F.R. Leavis calls the 'Great Tradition'. How far can they be located, for inspection, in the novels of her successors? Evidence for the continuity of the tradition can indeed be found in George Eliot, but together with great differences. The bond of eighteenth century idiom and decorum that unites Johnson and Jane Austen no longer exists in her prose. She has her own idiom, and her own intellectual equipment, highly individual and powerful. And she has her own imaginative equipment, using metaphor and simile, sometimes like a poet, sometimes clumsily. As one would expect, she attempts more ambitious effects. The following sentences from

[14] *Op. cit.*, Vol.1, Ch.2.

Daniel Deronda (Chapter 30), though they do not make one smile, are witty insofar as they exercise and entertain the mind with subtle shades of implication, as one surveys the behaviour of a singularly devious character. Grandcourt, about to marry Gwendolen, approaches his former mistress, Mrs Glasher, not only to break this fact to her but also to claim the jewels which have only been a temporary gift to her, and which on a former occasion she had refused to place in his keeping:

> . . . At that time Grandcourt had no motive which urged him to persist, and he had this grace in him, that the disposition to exercise power either by cowing or disappointing others or exciting in them a rage which they dared not express − a disposition which was active in him as other propensities became languid − had always been in abeyance before Lydia. A severe interpreter might say that the mere facts of their relation to each other, the melancholy position of this woman who depended on his will, made a standing banquet for his delight in dominating. But there was something else than this in his forbearance towards her, there was the surviving though metamorphosed effect of the power she had over him; and it was this effect, the fitful dull lapse towards solicitations that once had the zest now missing from life, which had again and again inclined him to espouse a familiar past rather than rouse himself to the expectation of novelty. But now novelty had taken hold of him and urged him to make the most of it.[15]

In passages such as these the English novel makes striking progress towards a modern psychological complexity. George Eliot is bold in her choice of material. She not only shows insight into the mind of a man, which Jane Austen did not attempt, and a man of libertine behaviour, but is able to see how libertinism might be combined with indolence and evasiveness. She recognises the role of habit and inertia in such a life. In her descriptions of Casaubon in *Middlemarch* her imaginative grasp of the special case, that of the learned but perilously isolated and ineffectual researcher, finds expression in metaphor, especially in a magnificent and celebrated paragraph in Chapter 29 where her compassion becomes most penetrative and eloquent. But an earlier passage, in

[15] *Daniel Deronda*, Harmondsworth 1967, p.389.

72

Chapter 7, is more to our purpose in that the theme is incongruity and the element of wit more pronounced. Mr Casaubon already feels, in the early days of his courtship, that his feelings towards Dorothea fall short of his expectations. Having decided 'to secure for himself the solace of female tendance for his declining years [he]

> . . . determined to abandon himself to the stream of feeling, and perhaps was surprised to find what an exceedingly shallow rill it was. As in droughty regions baptism by immersion could only be performed symbolically, so Mr Casaubon found that sprinkling was the utmost approach to a plunge which his stream would afford him; and he concluded that the poets had much exaggerated the force of masculine passion. Nevertheless, he observed with pleasure that Miss Brooke showed an ardent submissive affection which promised to fulfil his most agreeable previsions of marriage. It had once or twice crossed his mind that possibly there was some deficiency in Dorothea to account for the moderation of his abandonment; but he was unable to discern the deficiency, or to figure to himself a woman who would have pleased him better; so that there was clearly no reason to fall back upon but the exaggerations of human tradition.[16]

F.R. Leavis says of this passage that 'it is extraordinarily like something of the early satiric felicities' of E.M. Forster,[17] and the comparison with an inferior may prompt one to comment on the temptation of wit which sometimes caused Forster, in his turn, to fall to the level of his inferior, Lytton Strachey. Ought we to admire this passage, or rather to regard it as flippant, pedantic and inhuman? The water imagery may perhaps be a mid-Victorian signal to the reader, the only way in that period of referring to the inadequate sexuality of Mr Casaubon; but it becomes a laboured joke. As for the suggestion that he lacked the elementary power to recognise his own symptoms, but had to blame the poetic tradition, surely this is an unnecessary insult to his intelligence. To put it bluntly, George Eliot was not above showing off. Her insight into the strange predicament of this

[16] *Middlemarch*, London 1961, p.62. (Worlds' Classics edition).

[17] *The Great Tradition*, Harmondsworth 1966, p.75.

solitary, unlovable figure is impressive, and can be admirably sympathetic; but here she exploits it at his expense, and overdoes it.

To claim that George Eliot built upon the achievements of Jane Austen would be a misleading simplifcation. She had a wealth of sources, not all of them English and she had her own astonishing new departures. It would be difficult to put one's finger on any place where the intelligence and wit of the one owes anything specific to kindred gifts in the other. But the kinship is there. George Eliot without Jane Austen is unthinkable and, as Leavis notes, she admired her work profoundly.

The comparison between these examples from the two novelists does Jane Austen no harm. She describes more familiar states of mind, and embarks on no ambitious studies of tortuousness or deprivation in circumstances demanding special knowledge. She uses no poetic language. The scale of her attempts may be less, but so also are the hazards. The tone of her writing, which does not call attention to itself, preserves the dignity and freshness of her characters in places where George Eliot might have found it impossible to resist an obtrusive show of wit and analysis.

(2)

Jane Austen differs from her successors, George Eliot and others, in her treatment not only of individual characters but also of communities, while differing, as we have seen, from eighteenth century novelists, who lack a sense of the community. Mr Allworthy's relations with Black George and the Partridges cannot be seen as relations within a community. These minor characters exist episodically, as it were. They are there for the sake of incidents necessary to the plot, or to a moral structure within which the hero's virtues are exemplified; and the incidents are tailored for that purpose. Thus the Seagrims must be on the brink of starvation in order that Tom can be their clandestine succourer. We are not invited to ask how far Mr Allworthy should have been aware of their condition. It is not that kind of book. As with some fables and parables, only one point at a time can be entertained, and it may sometimes be at the expense of one character while the moral focus is on another. The sense of a community may seem much more evident in *Tristram Shandy*. The characters — Mr Shandy, Mrs Shandy, Uncle Toby, Trim, Obadiah, Susannah, Yorick and the other local worthies — do seem, in their different groupings in certain parts of the book, to exist together, entangled with each other's obsessions, crossing each other's paths or just sharing what E.M. Forster called a 'charmed stagnation'.[18] It would be impossible, indeed, without a full discussion, to do justice to the inwardness of Sterne's creation and the richness of the felt life captured within this essentially rhetorical structure. There is really no community in the sense in which it exists in *Emma*. One of the marks of the novel which has this dimension is that the minor characters are not present merely episodically, for the sake of plot or other artifice, but are felt to be really 'there', potentially part of the daily lives of the main characters. No social event in Jane Austen's novel can take place without the question arising in someone's mind of who is to be invited, and on any day of Emma's life the question might arise of visiting or not visiting Mrs and Miss Bates. But Jane Austen would never have written a book with a sub-title resembling that of *Middlemarch*: 'A Study of Provincial Life'. She did not see her subject-matter as 'society', with its conflicting interests and its 'pressures' on individuals. She attempted nothing remotely approaching a figure like Bulstrode, with his ramifying influence on Middlemarch politics and people, and the religious obsessions and labyrinthine casuistries that govern his relations with them. There are no public questions in her novels. No clergyman is seen in the light of his professional abilities or inadequacies. There are no conflicts or defeats arising out of the clash between personal relationships and cherished social projects. No landowner is known for his interest in, or his neglect of labourers' dwellings.

In his lecture on Tolstoy, F.R. Leavis makes a powerful claim for the great masters of fiction as the supreme interpreters of man in society:

> . . . A study of human nature is a study of social human nature, and the psychologist, sociologist, and social historian

[18] *Aspects of the Novel*, (1927), p.146.

aren't in it compared with the great novelists.[19]

In England George Eliot did more perhaps than anyone else to produce novels which justify such words. The novel in the late nineteenth and early twentieth centuries expanded in scope as more aspects of man's life in society were treated in fiction. But expansion in this respect does not necessarily lead to greater imaginative vitality. Henry James noted the extraordinary saturation in material and sociological detail in the fiction of his younger contemporaries, notably Bennett and Wells:

> . . . Each is ideally immersed in his own body of reference, in a closer notation, a sharper specification of the signs of life and consciousness in the human scene than the three or four generations before them had at all been moved to insist on.[20]

And while recognising that 'the author of *Clayhanger* has put down upon the table, in dense unconfused array, every fact required to make the life of the Five Towns press upon us and to make our sense of it, so full fed, content us,' he confesses to a 'dawning unrest', and asks: 'Yes, yes; but is this *all*? These are the circumstances of the interest. . .but where is the interest itself?'[21] Virginia Woolf's protest against the kind of realism achieved by Bennett and Wells, in her essay on 'Modern Fiction',[22] is well known.

Jane Austen, of course, made no conscious contribution to this development. If one looked for evidence in her work of the beginnings of such an approach, the theme on which she has most to say perhaps is that of social fluidity, the assimilation of wealthy tradesmen into the society of the gentry. Compared with Fanny Burney she does indeed illustrate this phenomenon in a positive way. The impossible Branghtons in *Evelina*, the grotesquely boorish Mr Briggs in *Cecilia*, are in the highest degree unassimilable, just as the Delviles in the latter novel are in the

[19] *'Anna Karenina' and other Essays*, London 1967, p.25.

[20] 'The Younger Generation', *Times Literary Supplement*, 19 March, 1914. Quoted in *Henry James and H.G. Wells*, ed., with an introduction by Leon Edel and Gordon N. Ray. London 1958, p.180.

[21] *Ibid* p.184.

[22] In *The Common Reader, First Series* (1925).

highest degree resistant even to much more moderate threats to their social exclusiveness. In the two novels by Jane Austen where this issue notably arises, *Pride and Prejudice* and *Emma*, assimilation does take place. *Pride and Prejudice* has the less genteel local community. Mr Bennet, a gentleman of property, has married the daughter of an attorney. Mrs Bennet's brother, Mr Gardiner, has settled in London in a respectable line of trade, and her sister has married her father's clerk, who has become his successor. Mr Bingley's sisters, apprehensive of Elizabeth's power over Darcy, make the most of these facts. But the class-consciousness of the Bingley young ladies is traceable to their own family history. They are 'of a respectable family in the north of England; a circumstance more deeply impressed upon their memories than that their brother's fortune and their own had been acquired by trade.'. (Chapter 4.) Elizabeth's 'intimate friend', Charlotte Lucas, is the daughter of a former tradesman who was knighted during his mayoralty and has retired from business. 'Unshackled by business', he occupies himself with being 'civil to all the world. . .By nature inoffensive, friendly and obliging, his presentation at St James's had made him courteous.' St James's has become his obsession. His wife, a 'very good sort of woman', is 'not too clever to be a valuable neighbour to Mrs Bennet.'. These people, with their foibles and faults of manner, are Elizabeth's family and friends. Can we say that Elizabeth, so much better than all of them, is entirely free from faults of manner? In the neighbourhood of Longbourn then birth and gentility have not been the most vital issues. But this is a novel in which bad manners may crop up anywhere. Mr Bennet's manners leave much to be desired, Lady Catherine's ill-breeding (Chapter 31) embarrasses Darcy, while Darcy on his first appearance is almost churlish, and his addresses to Elizabeth (Chapter 34) are resented by her, apart from being unacceptable on other grounds, as not 'gentleman-like'. He has been very outspoken about the inferiority of her family. Of Jane Austen's novels, *Pride and Prejudice* is the one in which the oppositions between social distinction and personal attraction are strongest, and it is remarkable for the cool recognition of the human facts that must be faced in such situations. Difficulties do not simply melt away when love triumphs. The novelist can even say, in the penultimate chapter, that the 'uncomfortable feelings' associated with unavoidable meetings detracted considerably, for Elizabeth and Darcy, from the pleasure of the 'season of courtship'. For example:

> Mrs Philips's vulgarity was another and perhaps a greater tax [i.e. than 'the parading and obsequious civility' of Sir William Lucas] on his forbearance; and though Mrs Philips, as well as her sister, stood in too much awe of him to speak with the familiarity which Bingley's good humour encouraged, yet, whenever she *did* speak she must be vulgar. . .Elizabeth did all she could, to shield him from the frequent notice of either, and was ever anxious to keep him to herself, and to those of her family with whom he might converse without mortification. . .

Jane Austen's heroines never seem to have doubts about the advantage of having advantages. When Elizabeth sees Pemberley (Chapter 43) the thought occurs to her that to be mistress of that property 'might be something', and near the end of the book (Chapter 59), in reply to Jane's question concerning the first dawning of her love for Darcy, she makes a joke, dating it from her first sight of those beautiful grounds. This may be nonsense, but Pemberley does express an ethos, a better taste than is evident at Rosings; and it is in such an environment that Mr Darcy, like his father, can earn a name for a distinguished goodness that raises him above ordinary men. Jane Austen herself clearly accepts Elizabeth's impression of Pemberley and all that she hears there about the Darcys, but she has already supplied the other side of the picture: Darcy's very imperfect adjustment to the world outside. There is never any doubt in *Mansfield Park* about the advantage to Fanny of having been adopted by Sir Thomas Bertram, and, frustrated as she is during her stay at her former Portsmouth home, she sees only one positive thing she can do; that is, secure the same advantage for her sister Susan. Mansfield Park has suffered a collapse of its way of life, and it might almost be said that Fanny – and Susan – will have as much to give as to gain during their subsequent stay there. The fact that these advantages, the order and peace that reign in Mansfield Park and not in Portsmouth, have a great deal to do with money, does not cloud her judgment of what is preferable. No part of Jane Austen's work has had a more dubious reception than that in which Fanny's experience in Portsmouth is recorded. A class of reader exists for whom Fanny's poor health, which deteriorates in Portsmouth, 'in the midst of closeness and noise. . . bad air, bad smells', offers just cause for antipathy. But Fanny's worst privation stems from the lack of feeling of her mother and father. Some readers are disturbed because she recognises faults in her mother, whom she sees as 'a partial, ill-judging parent, a dawdle, a slattern, who neither taught nor restrained her children, whose house was a scene of mismanagement and discomfort from beginning to end, and who had no talent, no conversation, no affection towards herself; no curiosity to know her better, no desire of her friendship. . .' (Chapter 38.) What right, it is argued, has Fanny to expect more than this? As if rights have anything to do with it, or questions of social equity. Jane Austen presents Fanny's situation, and shows no interest in questions of this kind. The fact is that the Price household is dead to any values that Fanny, or the reader, can respond to, and her sojourn there can only be an impoverishment for herself, with no opportunity to help. Readers have been shocked at Fanny's relief when Henry Crawford declines an invitation to dinner. To be ashamed of home, ashamed of poverty, where the alternative would have been a loyal affirmation, is one thing. But here no affirmation could be made; no basis exists on which she could conceivably second such an invitation. In matters of this kind Jane Austen shows a simple rightness of judgment, with no explaining or justifying. She does not even write as if this were a sensitive area. There are no general issues here, only particular ones.

Jane Austen shows no interest in social fluidity as a question, and as a fact in the lives of her characters it has an importance which is personal only. We never learn how the money was actually made when it was made in trade. Smollett, over forty years earlier, expresses through Matthew Bramble very specific disapproval of the sort of people who now infest the fashionable life of Bath:

> . . . Every upstart of fortune, harnessed in the trappings of the mode, presents himself at Bath, as in the very focus of observation. Clerks and factors from the East Indies, loaded with the spoils of plundered provinces; planters, negro drivers, and hucksters, from our American plantations, agents,

commissaries, and contractors, who have fattened, in two successive wars, on the blood of the nation; usurers, brokers, and jobbers of every kind. . .[23]

Jane Austen has nothing to say about the moral acceptability or otherwise of the relation of her newly rich characters to their material resources, nor do we know what her own attitude would have been had she been aware of all those economic relationships of the period which modern readers, and not only the most morally sensitive, must condemn with horror. Here we raise questions that are endless. All periods have different assumptions about how far and in what directions moral concern can go; and the attitude of good people to economic exploitation in the ages before societies became affluent and poverty could be regarded as an avoidable scandal, is beyond our power of imaginative retrieval. Jane Austen's total omission of these matters from her books may be seen as a manifestation of style and artistic tact. It enables her to treat the characters according to her own intimate knowledge of them. Jane Austen's good characters are good in specific ways, within a particular range, and their qualities are presented with such care and restraint that we are in no danger of forgetting the possibility of other moral perspectives, which in the fiction itself are irrelevant. If her novels sometimes make us reflect on the world outside them this is by no means a sign of inadequacy in her.

Ugly economic fact rears its head in one conspicuous place in *Emma*; and, characteristically, the focus is on Mrs Elton. Coming as she does from Bristol, she reacts sharply when Jane Fairfax seems to have made an allusion to the slave-trade: 'You quite shock me. . .I assure you, Mr Suckling was always rather a friend to the abolition' (Chapter 35.); which suggests indirectly that all is not well with the moneyed circle in which her own affluence has ripened.

Her novels, in general, are reticent concerning the details of the characters' style of living. But explicitness occurs notably in contexts that include Mrs Elton, and are an expression of her vulgar invidiousness. The barouche-landau of the Sucklings, 'the

[23] *The Expedition of Humphry Clinker.* Matthew Bramble to Dr Lewis, Bath, April 23.

poor attempt at rout-cakes, and there being no ice in the High-bury card parties', her resolution to give a superior party, 'in which her card tables should be set out with their separate candles and unbroken packs in the true style'(Chapter 34.), and with extra waiters to carry round refreshments at the appropriate times: all this, with the addition of the 'wax-candles in the schoolroom' in Mrs Bragge's establishment, an inducement for Jane Fairfax to become a governess there, is quite untypical of Jane Austen. Anything slightly amiss with the Coles, who are only 'moderately genteel', is discreetly left unspecified. But where Mrs Elton is concerned the intense animosity of the portrayal cannot satisfy itself without fulness of illustrative detail.

Within a generation or two of Jane Austen the vogue had changed. The early Victorian Thackeray, in his portrayal of society, enriches his surfaces with lavish details of manner and visual effect. The toilette and dress of Major Pendennis,[24] the in-continent profusion of the Claverings' drawing room[25] are material for great set pieces, compared with which Jane Austen's treatment of her society appears very reticent and frugal. Scott, with his historical and Scottish local colour, played a crucial part in this development, and Balzac applied local colour to the con-temporary scene. The question of whether Frank Churchill dressed with a certain amount of Regency foppery is never raised, whereas very specific details of Pendennis's 'wonderful shooting-jackets, with remarkable buttons', his 'gorgeous velvet waistcoats, with richly embroidered cravats, and curious linen',[26] his style of entertaining, and other tokens of expensive living at Oxbridge are lavishly exhibited. An element of generality, something of the spirit of the eighteenth century, survives in Jane Austen. The fine particularisation of behaviour in her work is with respect to matters of morality and taste which depend only occasionally on realisation in terms of these material incidentals.

*   *   *

In liberating the novel from its inveterate dependence on

[24] *Pendennis*, Ch.7.
[25] *Ibid*. Ch.37.
[26] *Ibid*. Ch.18, 19.

violence and extreme situations Jane Austen, as we have seen, had to be an innovator in the art of plotting to find alternative means of keeping a novel alive. At the same time the theme of sex, often associated with these extremes in earlier fiction, is greatly reduced in scope. Jane Austen is at one with other writers of her age in treating the subject with great reserve. The sexual theme had served eighteenth century authors well, and now those of the nineteenth century were obliged to find new kinds of involvement for the moral life. Inevitably, a 'domestic' strain in fiction developed, with domestic virtues, and compared with the nineteenth century fiction of continental countries, with its bolder range, the Anglo-Saxon achievement came for a time to be regarded as gravely limited. But in the last generation or so the novels of Anglo-Saxon moral awareness, with George Eliot's work in the centre, have received their full due, and the limited treatment of sex has been much less frequently harped upon. Jane Austen's contribution to the development of new fictional situations was very important. One theme that might be specified concerns the implications of meddling with another person's life. Emma does this with Harriet, Rowland Mallett with Roderick Hudson, Olive Chancellor with Verena in *The Bostonians*: all in very different ways, of course. It is the central theme of *Great Expectations*. Not that one would claim for Jane Austen that she starts themes which other writers consciously take over from her, but rather that she sets a standard of inventiveness in a new phrase of the history of the novel. The question of what an intelligent and aspiring girl, whose first thought is not marital happiness, can do with her life, becomes a most fruitful subject for George Eliot and Henry James. It does not take this form in Jane Austen's work, because she subscribes to the tradition which provides marital happiness for all her heroines. But the position of some of these heroines, before their destiny becomes clear, raises issues that were to become more sharply focused later in the century. The spectacle of Emma, at a loose end, finding something to do but not advisedly, and then becoming involved, with little power of control, in a confusing series of social events and misunderstandings, with her cleverness and high spirits often wrongly engaged, may not have seemed in 1815 to have implications calling for fuller development; but George Eliot's achievement helps us to see more in Jane Austen's. The eighteenth century heroine's main task was to defend herself from sexual violence or treachery, parental tyranny and the pesterings of the vulgar. For several of Jane Austen's heroines problems other than these are posed, but as they are solved by marriage they do not seem to call insistently for discussion. In some cases the girl is too intelligent for her circle, highly critical but unable to do anything on her own initiative. Elizabeth marries Darcy, which rescues her from a prospect which has become dispiriting enough, if we needed to take it seriously. In *The Mill on the Floss* George Eliot chooses a heroine for whom deprivation is a bitter reality. The predicament of Jane Fairfax has much in common with that of Gwendolen Harleth: both are rescued by marriage from servitude of a governess. But Jane's marriage, which we hope will be happy, is not part of the story. The miseries of unhappy marriage are among George Eliot's ambitious themes. Jane Austen's sense of reality makes us recognise what could have happened if all had not gone well with her heroines, though she has no need to stress it. An alternative fate can be envisaged in some detail. In the story of Anne Elliot, her last and one of her most original creations, the alternative to happy marriage is actually experienced, and we have a painful impression of the utterly cramping and frustrating conditions in which she must live, until the change in her fortunes makes possible an even deeper happiness than a less mature heroine might have been capable of. Some George Eliot or Henry James heroines would have responded differently to their fate. Anne just lives patiently within the limited framework provided by her largely unsympathetic family. But she has developed her virtues of fortitude and realism, she has intelligence and self-knowledge, and her love for Wentworth has never died; and when these qualities have their chance to manifest themselves in a series of episodes in the later part of the novel, the effect is extraordinarily impressive. Her words to Captain Harville on the subject of a woman's love have the power of a great affirmation, going beyond anything in Jane Austen's earlier treatment of love. Unlike the heroines of these later writers, Anne, after suffering so much as a result of conventional advice, does not break with the conventional view of a girl's duty to her mentors. The later heroines tend to be reckless and independent, and new views of life are in the air. Anne's total lack of protest against the conditions imposed by her society is admirably in character and in keeping with the unity of the book, but her case stretches the convention almost to breaking point. Jane Austen did much then to create the conditions within which a new kind of heroine could come into being.

In our time the seriousness and sophistication of Jane Austen's work are not in question, and indeed there may be a tendency among some modern readers to overemphasise her astringency. D.W. Harding's essay on 'regulated hatred'[27] in Jane Austen produced a valuable reaction, necessary at the time, but astringency can become a fashionable quality like anything else. If the term 'domestic' applied to fiction is a term of reproach it has to be admitted that Jane Austen in some measure incurs it. The role of Mr Woodhouse provides a test case. There seems to be no doubt that Emma's care for her father is absolutely central to her life, and that her cherishing of him in all his eccentricities embodies a moral principle of importance to the author and to the great mass of her readers. Mark Schorer's comment on him as 'the destructive. . . malingering egotist'[28] amounts to a refusal to accept Jane Austen's presentation. Marvin Mudrick goes further:

. . . He is not agreeable. He is, in fact, a nuisance, with his gruel, his hypochondria. . . Mr Woodhouse — after long years of invalidism, of being coddled by his daughter — is an idiot. . . . [He] is the living — barely living — excuse for Emma's refusal to commit herself to the human world.[29]

The last sentence, at least, is nonsense. When Mr Woodhouse hears the disturbing news of Emma's intention to marry, and uses all his customary arguments to dissuade her, Emma's desire to 'commit herself to the human world', and her affection for her father, are both most convincingly and delightfully manifest: 'But it would not do. Emma hung about him affectionately, and smiled, and said it must be so.' (Chapter 53.) Mr Woodhouse is always treated with great respect and consideration by Mr Knightley, who never gives evidence of any criticism or impatience. Nor

[27] In *Scrutiny*, VIII, March 1940.
[28] 'The Humiliation of Emma Woodhouse', *Literary Review*, Summer 1959. Reprinted in Lodge, p.182.
[29] *Jane Austen: Irony as Defence and Discovery*, Berkeley and Los Angeles 1968, pp.195-6.

is the reader ever invited to be irreverent. In the passage at the beginning of Chapter 9, where Emma and Harriet occupy themselves with riddles, one sees that this is just about his intellectual level ('So many clever riddles as there used to be when he was young. . .'), and although the passage contains a sufficient indication of Emma's culpability in relation to Harriet, the moral note, as we saw earlier, is easy enough to tone in with Mr Woodhouse's innocent participation. To have allowed Mr Woodhouse to be in any way relegated, deprived of respect, would have been contrary to the good manners and humanity of the novelist as well as of the characters. Marvin Mudrick[30] says that we can sympathise with Mr John Knightley when he loses his temper with Mr Woodhouse, and he is partly right. A safety valve may be necessary, though forbearance is the general rule. On the whole Lionel Trilling's comment on Mudrick is appropriate: 'Only a modern critic, Professor Mudrick, would think to call Mr Woodhouse an idiot and an old woman: in the novel he is called "the kind-hearted, polite old gentleman".'[31] But Trilling overshoots the mark when he refers to Mr Woodhouse and Miss Bates as 'sacred fools of a special and transcendent kind. . . of such is the kingdom of heaven.'[32] It is enough to say that they provide a test of good feeling in the life of families and small communities.

A character like Miss Bates would have been fair game for a caricaturist in eighteenth century fiction. There was no provision in any novel before Jane Austen for a treatment giving her equality with the principal characters. Not that she enjoys total equality. In endowing her with a special idiom of rambling speech Jane Austen follows to some extent the eighteenth century manner with comic minor characters, and, of course, socially she belongs to the category of 'less worthy females' who come to the party at the Coles after dinner. But she has equality to the extent that, unlike characters of her kind in eighteenth century fiction (one thinks of Tabitha Bramble in *Humphry Clinker*), she does not exist merely as a figure of fun, a conventional foil or satellite. She is there in her own right, and the Bates's cottage is as

[30] *Ibid*. pp.195-6.

[31] *Ibid*. p.165.

[32] *Ibid*. p.162.

much a focus of human concern, even without Jane Fairfax, as any other place in Highbury. The treatment accorded to her in the community to which, however humbly, she belongs, has its slight documentary interest. On the evening of the Coles' dinner party it occurs to Mrs Weston that, in view of Jane Fairfax's state of health, their carriage should be sent for her and for Miss Bates; but they are too late. Mr Knightley, departing to Emma's great satisfaction from his usual custom of walking, has done so, as it turns out later, in order to provide transport for these ladies. The implication would seem to be that Miss Bates, in the past, has always walked, and that even Mr Knightley would not necessarily have made a custom of sending his carriage. The point is a minor one, but has its interest for those of us today who have no motor car, and profit regularly from the well-organised kindness of friends on such occasions. But Mr Knightley keeps in touch with the Bateses and is both generous and considerate with his gifts. On the whole they are happy in their friends. Emma alone fails in this respect, with her uncharitable satire and reluctance to pay visits. It is surely remarkable that the humble figure of Miss Bates should be the occasion for the great turning point in Emma's moral development. Rudeness to her has that degree of importance. This shift in moral sensibility between eighteenth century fiction and *Emma* has received less attention than other movements of sensibility in this age of literary change. One of the routes stemming from *Emma* leads to *Cranford*, and beyond; but this is a minor tradition, too near to the minor tradition of Jane Austen criticism from which recent generations have rescued her, so perhaps the point should not be stressed.

Jane Austen's novels were written in a domestic atmosphere, read aloud in the family and commented on by friends and relations. She made a collection of these opinions, and they are as ordinary as one would expect from people who have no special experience of critical reading. She has always had an abundance of such readers, and although she must have realised how much more there was in her novels than her general readership would appreciate, there is a sense in which she wrote for them. Not to have written for them, or to have done so with divisively ironical reserves, would have been contrary to what we know of her character and dealings with people. It is characteristic of her subtlest passages that they are really very straightforward. Their subtlety lies in the fact that they are truer than we first realised. She puts her readers at their ease. 'Emma Woodhouse, handsome, clever, and rich, with a comfortable home and happy dispostiion. . .', may or may not owe its simplicity to her humorous awareness of more elaborate introductions of characters in earlier novels, but certainly, as an opening, it has the merit of making all her readers, or all those to whom the book is read aloud in the family, equal at the outset. Jane Austen can achieve this disarming quality, and, at the same time, the density of implication of the greatest fiction.

SELECT BIBLIOGRAPHY

Text

Emma was first published by John Murray in December 1815 in three volumes. The title page is dated 1816. Quotations from *Emma* and other works by Jane Austen are taken from R.W. Chapman's edition of 'The Novels of Jane Austen' published by Oxford University Press.

Critical works

WAYNE C. BOOTH: *The Rhetoric of Fiction* (Chicago, Illinois: University of Chicago Press, 1961

F.W. BRADBROOK: *Jane Austen and her Predecessors* (London: Cambridge University Press, 1966.)

Emma (London: Arnold, 1961.)

R.W. CHAPMAN: *Jane Austen: Facts and Problems* (1948). (Oxford: Clarendon Press, 1970.)

D.D. DEVLIN: *Jane Austen and Education* (London: Macmillan, 1975.)

JOHN HALPERIN (editor): *Jane Austen: Bi-Centenary Essays* (London: Cambridge University Press, 1975.) (Contains Select Bibliography)

D.W. HARDING: 'Regulated Hatred: An Aspect of Jane Austen' (*Scrutiny*, Vol. VIII, 1940.)

BARBARA HARDY: *A Reading of Jane Austen* (London: Peter Owen, 1975.)

ARNOLD KETTLE: *An Introduction to the English Novel*, Vol.I (London : Hutchinson, 1951.)

Q.D. LEAVIS: 'A Critical Theory of Jane Austen's Writings' (in four parts: *Scrutiny*, Vol.X 1941; Vol.X 1942; Vol.XII 1944). Reprinted in *A Selection from Scrutiny*, compiled by F.R. Leavis (London: Cambridge University Press, 1968, Vol. 2.)

MARY LASCELLES: *Jane Austen and her Art* (London: Oxford University Press, 1939.)

ROBERT LIDDELL: *The Novels of Jane Austen* (London: Longmans, 1963.)

DAVID LODGE (editor): *Emma: A Casebook* (London: Macmillan, 1968.) Contains essays by Arnold Kettle, Marvin Mudrick, Edgar F. Shannon, Jr., Lionel Trilling, Mark Shorer, R.E. Hughes, Wayne Booth, Malcolm Bradbury, W.J. Harvey.)

MARVIN MUDRICK: *Jane Austen: Irony as Defence and Discovery* (Berkeley and Los Angeles: University of California Press, 1968.)

B.C. SOUTHAM: *Jane Austen's Literary Manuscripts* (Oxford: Clarendon Press, 1964.)

LIONEL TRILLING: '*Emma* and the Legend of Jane Austen'. Introduction to Riverside edition of *Emma*; reprinted in *Beyond Culture* (1965) (Harmondsworth: Penguin Books, 1967)

ANDREW H. WRIGHT: *Jane Austen's Novels: A Study in Structure* (1953). (London: Chatto and Windus, 1961 Revised Edition.)